CHICKEN SOUP
FOR THE
NURSE'S SOUL

Second Dose

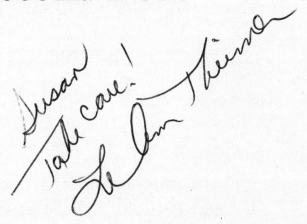

Chicken Soup for the Nurse's Soul Second Dose
More Stories to Honor and Inspire Nurses
Jack Canfield, Mark Victor Hansen, LeAnn Thieman

Published by Backlist, LLC,
a unit of Chicken Soup for the Soul Publishing, LLC. www.chickensoup.com

Front cover design by Andrea Perrine Brower
Originally published in 2007 by Health Communications, Inc.

Back cover and spine redesign by Pneuma Books, LLC

Distributed to the booktrade by Simon & Schuster. SAN: 200-2442

Publisher's Cataloging-in-Publication Data
(Prepared by The Donohue Group)

Chicken soup for the nurse's soul : second dose : more stories to honor and inspire nurses / [compiled by] Jack Canfield, Mark Victor Hansen, [and] LeAnn Thieman.

  p. : ill. ; cm.

  Originally published: Deerfield Beach, FL : Health Communications, c2007.
  ISBN: 978-1-62361-062-3

  1. Nursing--Anecdotes. 2. Nursing--Popular works. 3. Nurses--Anecdotes. 4. Anecdotes. I. Canfield, Jack, 1944- II. Hansen, Mark Victor. III. Thieman, LeAnn.

RT61 .C3762 2012
610.73   2012944406

PRINTED IN THE UNITED STATES OF AMERICA
on acid free paper
21 20 19 18 17 16 15 14   03 04 05 06 07 08 09 10

CHICKEN SOUP
FOR THE
NURSE'S SOUL

Second Dose

More Stories to Honor and Inspire Nurses

Jack Canfield
Mark Victor Hansen
LeAnn Thieman

Backlist, LLC, a unit of
Chicken Soup for the Soul Publishing, LLC
Cos Cob, CT
www.chickensoup.com

Contents

v

5. BEYOND THE CALL OF DUTY

6. LESSONS

7. MATTER OF PERSPECTIVE

10. THANK YOU

Introduction

Nearly 1 million nurses have been touched by the stories in the first edition of *Chicken Soup for the Nurse's Soul*. As a professional speaker, I am blessed to talk to tens of thousands of them. Over and over again they tell me how the stories bolstered them . . . how they read just the right story on just the right day, just when they needed it. Some nurses keep the book in their locker at work, others read it together at the beginning of shift report, still others keep it as a ready "reference" at the nurse's desk.

It is my hope that you will keep it handy at your bedside, or in your bathroom or break room (some days they're the same thing!) and enjoy a dose of inspiration x1 daily and p.r.n. These stories of hope and healing will remind you why you entered this honorable profession . . . and why you stay. Let them fill you with hope and pride and strength to continue your courageous, compassionate caring.

For every hand you've held, for every life you've touched, we thank you.

With love and admiration,
LeAnn Thieman

1

DEFINING MOMENTS

Life is a succession of lessons which must be lived to be understood.

Helen Keller

Hope

Appetite, with an opinion of attaining, is called
hope; the same, without such opinion, despair.

Thomas Hobbes

"Good thing you got him here! Any longer and we would have had to remove part of his bowel. He has an inguinal hernia . . . if it had strangulated . . . " I didn't understand the medical jargon. The doctor was explaining my baby's condition, but he might as well have been speaking French.

Johnny was seven months old when he screamed uncontrollably, despite all my efforts to appease him. I knew something was seriously wrong. I bolted into the emergency department. The ER doctor examined him and the next thing I knew I was signing papers for emergency surgery.

Fear numbed me as I inwardly prayed that Johnny would be okay. God was the only glimmer in my dismal life back then. At age twenty-three, I was struggling to support my three children. Our marriage was failing and we were separated. Again.

I'd survived mostly on government assistance since the birth of my first child, who was four years old. I'd quit high school during my twelfth year and later obtained my GED. My work history was sketchy, but I longed to be financially stable. I prayed earnestly for direction.

I spent as much time as I could with Johnny and I hated leaving him to be tended by strangers. While visiting, I noticed one of his care-providers was dressed in green while the rest wore the traditional white. I wanted to ask her why, but I was still dazed by everything and did not have the emotional energy for idle inquisitions.

One day I watched as she busied herself taking Johnny's temperature. My curiosity overwhelmed me. "Why are you wearing a green dress?"

"I'm a nursing student," she replied.

"What school do you attend?" I continued, just making conversation. She told me all about a one-year federally funded program.

"How do you become a part of this program?" I asked.

The friendly student smiled eagerly. "Let me tell you about becoming a nurse."

With pride and enthusiasm she gave me a detailed account of what was necessary. I had never considered a nursing career, although since leaving high school, I thirsted for knowledge. As I listened to her, I felt the dying flame of hope rekindling. *Could I do this?*

During the following weeks I completed the list of prerequisites she shared with me. Everything was coming together fine. Then I discovered that having your own transportation was a requirement. "But I don't have a car," I explained to the program director. They could only accept thirty-two students and they screened carefully trying to select those most likely to graduate. She studied my face in silence.

"I will give you two months to get one," she said hopefully.

Yes! I thought while thanking God for victory. My heart

fluttered with excitement. I was scheduled to begin classes in two months.

"I'm going to be a nurse!" I proudly proclaimed to my family.

Their laughter was biting.

"Do you think you can be a nurse? You've never been around sick people."

"I can see you fainting at the first sight of blood!" my mother added.

When I'd quit school it was no surprise to them because no one in my family had ever graduated. They meant no harm, but their thoughtless cruelty fueled my determination to succeed. *I'm going to finish nursing school if only to show them,* I pledged to myself.

On the starting date I woke with excitement, then gasped at the dramatic weather changes. Heavy snow covered the trees and roads. Fallen tree branches covered portions of the streets as far as I could see. I had slept through the worst ice storm in the history of our county. The radio recited a long list of closings. I was sure my school was among them, but I called to confirm. "No, we are open for classes," the receptionist informed me. My father agreed to take me and came without a murmur.

We gathered in one classroom sharing our nursing aspirations. When I explained how I learned about the program, everyone was amazed that I started the same year that I applied. "I've been on the waiting list for two years!" was the common response from others. This confirmed what I already knew: this career move was orchestrated by God.

School demanded rigorous discipline. My children were ten months, two, and four. I had two in diapers and one in preschool. After a full day at school, I looked forward to spending time with them. By the time I got them fed, bathed, and prepared for bed, I was exhausted. I gathered my thick medical texts to prepare for study and was asleep in seconds. It was God's grace and my thirst for knowledge that enabled me to earn good grades.

Things went well until the ninth month when I experienced medical problems and my doctor recommended bed rest. There was no way for me to miss classes and maintain passing grades.

"Take some time off to get better and return next year," the director said. I was devastated, having anticipated graduation in only three months. I had invested too much to give up and was ready for my struggling to end.

With regained health I returned the following year. I was appalled to learn that only three months' credit was granted for the previous nine months of toil. I pushed my anger aside and forged ahead. I worked harder than ever for nine months and I graduated, with my family smiling proudly in the audience.

After passing the state-mandated test, I became a licensed practical nurse. I submitted applications to all the local hospitals. When I talked to other classmates, they all had dates scheduled for orientation. I had not heard a thing. I debated whether to call and check on my application. Hesitantly, I phoned the hospital where I really wanted to work. "I'm wondering if you've been trying to call me . . . I'm in and out often . . ."

"Yes we have," the human resource staffer responded.

Thus began my nursing career.

A few years later I entered college to become a registered nurse. That was twenty-three years ago and I thank God every day for calling me to serve others in this way.

Recently, as I cared for my patient, a weary-looking young woman visitor asked, "Is it hard to be a nurse?"

I detected a glimmer of hope in her eyes.

I smiled eagerly. "Let me tell you about becoming a nurse . . ."

Jeri Darby

Pilar

Even as a small child, I remember wanting to be a nurse. I dreamed of being all dressed in starched white with a cap perched neatly on my head. I always had a little plastic nurse bag, filled with the tricks of the trade. I nursed all my dolls, teddy bears, pets, and even my brother and sister when I could corner them to play with me.

Then one person seemed to seal this desire in my life. When I was eight, my mother was seriously injured and spent a month in a hospital that was forty miles from our little ranching community. She spent part of the critical time in a burn center and then was moved to a medical unit in a tall red brick building. We missed Mama so, but neither my brother, sister, nor myself were fourteen yet, so we weren't allowed to visit.

Dad took us to the hospital and we stood on the lawn outside to see a blurred wave from our mother through a high-up window as she lay in her bed.

Dad assured us that a special nurse was taking care of Mom. Pilar was a gentle person who tenderly cared for Mom's broken body. Then she'd sit at her bedside and read the Bible to her when my mother could not hold a book for herself. She would push the bed nearer the window so my mom could see us better on days we came to "visit." But Mom missed her kids and her kids didn't understand.

One day we went to town with Dad on some errands and planned to stop and wave up at my mother. We stepped up to the brick building and my dad went inside to tell Pilar we were waiting for a glimpse of Mom through the window. But instead of going into my mother's room, Pilar took off down the back stairway, came outside to the three of us, and said, "Be very quiet and follow me."

We went back to the stairs and snuck up to the proper floor. Pilar opened the door and glanced down the hall. Like a protective mother hen, she expertly and quietly guided us hurriedly into my mother's room and shut the door, leaning against it like a guard. And suddenly, after weeks of only seeing her wave, there was my mom. She was in slings and bandages, but we could touch her and feel her mothering hands. I'm sure we were much too loud in our excitement, but it was too good to hold inside. My dad stood quietly and blew his nose.

The next week, we were huddled on the lawn under Mom's window when Pilar appeared again and repeated the wonderful words, "Follow me!" We tiptoed up the back staircase and she secretly herded us into Mama's room. There on the bedside stand sat a chocolate cake with fudge frosting. We giggled and munched with Dad and Mom and ate until it was gone.

Eventually, my mother came home. She talked often through the years about Pilar, and I realized what an impact she had made on my mother and on me.

She was exactly the nurse I wanted to be.

Terry Evans

Memories of Polo

Death may be the greatest of all human blessings.

Socrates

Every time I smell the sweet pungent fragrance of Polo aftershave, memories take me back to the trauma intensive care unit. Almost twenty years of nursing and uncountable numbers of patients fade away when that sweet aroma floods my senses. Once again I am standing at Roy's bedside.

Nursing was new to me then, but the unit wasn't. I had worked as a nurse assistant at night and attended nursing school clinicals in the unit during the day. New graduates weren't usually hired into the ICU, but to me it was home and, with the staff's blessings, my first job as a graduate R.N.

I had little experience with death. It wasn't discussed much in school. The doctors acted as if it was a dragon to be defeated at all costs. The experienced nurses told me death wasn't the enemy. I didn't really understand what they were trying to say.

Until Roy.

What he taught me about death brings a hot rush of tears as I write this. But nurses aren't supposed to cry, are they?

"So sad," Donna told the charge nurse as I walked up. Twenty years of nursing had etched a permanent look of concern on her grandmotherly old face. "You're young, Sharon," she said. "Maybe Roy will talk to you."

"Why is he here?" I asked.

"Motorcycle accident," she replied. "I'll watch your patients, you go visit Roy."

Time hasn't dampened the rush of raw teenage emotion that met me at the door to Roy's room. The tracheostomy tube didn't affect his ability to communicate the anger and frustration he felt.

"I hate this place. I hate you. I want to go home," he mouthed as I walked in.

His greasy, matted hair was plastered against his scalp. His thin, gangly body was lost in a jumble of wrinkled sheets and tubes. His eyes were dark brown and challenging. Fear and pain mixed in with his message, but what fifteen-year-old boy would admit that? His face was covered with acne and a sparse, peach-fuzz trace of beard. He reminded me of the abandoned puppy I had found on the side of the road. He also reminded me of my cousin Mark who'd been so excited and proud about the whiskers he had grown (about twelve hairs as I recall).

I looked seriously at Roy. "You sure can't go out looking like this," I said. "You need a bath and a shave, or are you planning on growing a beard?"

Roy looked at me wide-eyed. He rubbed his hand across his chin and grinned. The way his expression changed told me he was sure his beard must be thick . . . a man's beard.

"A bath and a shave," he mouthed. "I use Polo after-shave," he informed me proudly.

"Polo it is then."

The bath, shave, clean sheets, and pain medicine sealed our friendship. Bathtime became our nightly routine. Roy would drift off to sleep with the sweet smell of Polo filling his dreams with other places and situations far removed from the reality of his hospital room. Polo's aroma lingered on my uniform and silently followed me as I worked.

Roy's accident was a tragedy. He was from a small mountain town far from the hospital. His friend had a new motorcycle that Roy wanted to try. His dad said no, but Roy, in typical teenage style, rode it anyway, wrecking almost immediately. His chest was crushed against a tele-phone pole.

The left lung was unrepairable, the right lung damaged. Angry with his son and devastated by the doctors' dire predictions, Roy's dad refused to visit. Roy's mom didn't drive.

The sweet smell of Polo and the sound of MTV filled Roy's room on my night shift. He loved baseball and bragged about his school team. We decorated his room with baseball posters and balloons. As he became more cooperative, the day shift began to spoil him too. Roy told me he had a younger sister. We couldn't replace his fam-ily, but we were determined to make sure he felt special and loved.

The last week of Roy's short life was a blur of activity as doctors and nurses worked to save him. *Nurses don't cry,* I told myself as I charted on Roy's last night. My tears fell anyway, ignoring my orders to keep a professional perspective.

"I'm not assigning you patients tonight," the charge nurse said in report. "Roy has been asking for you and there is not much we can do now. He's not expected to live until morning."

"Does he know?" I asked, blinking back tears.

No one answered me.

Roy and I had never talked about death. We both were still young enough to think that death only happened to someone else.

As Roy began to die, he held my hand so tightly my fingers became numb. He begged me not to leave his side. I held his hand and whispered about baseball and a place called heaven where he would be free of pain, while my colleagues worked frantically, and he slowly suffocated.

"Good-bye Roy," I told him as I bathed his now cold body and splashed Polo on his face one last time. As the sweet aroma filled his room, I began to feel better. Roy taught me what nursing school didn't.

Sometimes death is the cure, and good nurses do cry.

Sharon T. Hinton

Nurse Nancy

The man who has confidence in himself gains the confidence of others.

Hasidic Saying

My strong sense of what I wanted to be when I grew up came from memories of my first five years of childhood spent in an orphanage in Ohio. I fondly remember a nurse who was my friend there. She was my "Angel of Mercy," my real-life Nurse Nancy. She wore a white hat, starched white uniform, tight white hose, white shoes, and a blue cape. How I loved my nurse. She told me stories, tickled me, made me giggle and laugh, and filled my bath full of huge colored bubbles. My nurse was my hero and I wanted to be just like her.

When I was blessed by being adopted, my parents must have known my devotion to this nurse. I arrived at my new home to find a gift placed in my very own bed—a nursing outfit: a white uniform, cap, and cape, plus shots, Band-Aids, and a stethoscope. Everything I would need to fulfill my role as Nurse Nancy.

Remember Golden Books? As a child I treasured them.

My favorite was titled, no surprise, *Nurse Nancy*. This treasured book read, "Nancy liked to play with dolls. She liked to play mother. Best of all, she liked to play nurse." That was me as a child. I bandaged my dolls, my dog, my brother! Anyone who would sit long enough was nursed. I gave M&Ms to my patients for pills, which, needless to say, kept me busy playing nurse. All the neighborhood children lined up for my care. I, like Nurse Nancy, kept logbooks with recorded names of my patients, such as Baby 1, Baby 2. Listed diseases included, but were not limited to, sick, fever, cold, and measles.

Make-believe days have passed. I have been a "real" nurse for thirty-plus years.

Of all my years as a nurse, the greatest blessing this career gave me happened sixteen years ago when my husband and I spent three weeks in Romania waiting to adopt our twin sons. Because they were six weeks premature, we had to wait for them to gain weight before we could take them home. The doctor was reluctant to release these tiny babies to new, inexperienced parents. Needless to say, we were eager to return home with our twins.

One day as I talked to their nurses, I thanked them for their care. Despite our language barrier, I was able to see and feel the genuine concern they had for our soon-to-be sons. I witnessed again the reputation nurses have for caring and compassion . . . as far-reaching as an orphanage in Ohio to an orphanage in Romania. In this conversation, I revealed that I, too, was a nurse. At that moment the nurses left the room.

Shortly thereafter, through the doors burst an exuberant doctor, and in his marked Romanian accent he called out, "Why did you not tell me you were a nurse? I release your sons to your care today, Nurse Nancy!"

Nancy Barnes

Welcome to War

War *is a series of catastrophes that results in a* *victory.*

Georges Clemenceau

I was twenty-two years old when, on a whim, I volunteered to go to Vietnam. It was the autumn of 1970 and,
despite my age, I was considered an experienced pediatric
nurse, to be assigned to the U.S. Army's only children's
hospital in Quang Tri.

It was a long flight overseas with only a brief stop in
Hawaii. Some soldier, barely old enough, offered to buy
me a drink at the airport bar. I was so impressed with the
fun, the camaraderie, and just plain courtesy I observed
on that trip over. A naturally shy person, I was overwhelmed by how many men came over to meet me. They
made me feel as if they were honored to be in my presence
because I had volunteered to care for them. All throughout my weeks of basic training I had noticed the near rev-
erence with which we nurses were treated.

I landed in Vietnam at night, at the Bien Hoa airstrip

outside of Saigon. I'll never forget that night, my first introduction to warfare. From the bus we heard thundering guns, saw the eerie lightning, and witnessed the extreme poverty of the war's victims. They huddled in cardboard huts, their fragile homes advertising corporate giants like General Electric, Ford, and Westinghouse.

I wondered what was in store for me.

A few days later I was flown north, to within five miles of the demilitarized zone separating South Vietnam from our enemy, the Communist Republic of North Vietnam. The airport near the hospital where I was to work was a busy place; military jets were taking off all around me. I had never felt quite so alone. Then I heard someone call "Lieutenant Burghart?" I found myself surrounded by several young American soldiers from the 18th surgical hospital and the 237th Dustoff unit. They had a tradition of greeting new nurses with a helicopter ride, carrying them across the street.

However, one man in the Dustoff unit scoffed, "Flying across the street to pick up a nurse is a waste of time!"

Another whispered to me, "Private Geoffrey Morris's unit just lost three helicopters and their crews."

No wonder he didn't have much room for frivolity in war.

It wasn't long before I heard from Geoff Morris again. He was strolling down the hospital corridor soon after my arrival and heard me asking someone to donate blood for one of my young patients. When I was unsuccessful, he watched as I took blood from my own arm for the child.

Thirty-five years have gone by since then, and Geoff still likes to tell our four children that that was the moment he fell in love with me.

Emily Morris

Confessions of a CNO

Remember this—that there is a proper dignity and proportion to be observed in the performance of every act of life.

Marcus Aurelius Antoninus

As I connect with all of the wonderful nurses that I have had the privilege to work with over thirty-five years in administration, and ask them why they became nurses, the answers are inevitably similar. "I want to help people," "I wanted to be a nurse like my mom," "I want to feel valuable to the greater good or the community." My journey to nursing was not so altruistic. I must confess, I wanted to be a dancer, not a nurse. My goal was to live and dance professionally in New York City. A friend who was studying nursing convinced me that if I took a couple of years off from dancing to obtain my nursing degree, I could have a good job between shows and I wouldn't have to wait tables like other striving actresses and dancers. I thought her suggestion was a great idea, even though I felt that my place in life was to make people happy by entertaining them. But when I began working in the hospital as a nurse, my life was transformed.

I realized that as a performer I made people happy for a few minutes but I did not have a meaningful impact on their lives. Nurses cared about people, whereby most performers cared about themselves and their next job. It began to frustrate me to observe the value that society continually placed on performers as evidenced by the money and fame that they received. It undervalued the "true heroes"—the nurses.

I knew that I would never leave nursing to dance again when I began working in critical care as a new nurse. I received the call from the emergency department that we were getting a level-one trauma patient. A student nurse on her way home from a study group totaled her car close to our hospital. In those days, very long ago, seat belts were not promoted as they are today, and she was ejected out the front window, under the car, which then exploded. Surprisingly, she did not suffer severe burns, but her skull was crushed. Soon after surgery, brain activity ceased. Her mom, tormented by the turn of events, truly believed that her daughter was going to recover. Staff members did not share the same level of optimism but supported the family in their decision to maintain life support until they were ready to make that difficult decision. Determined that she would recover, her mom refused the option for organ donation. She did agree, however, that if her daughter arrested we would not "code" her or perform unnecessary heroics.

I had a special connection to this patient since she was only two years younger than I and shared the same interest in nursing.

About two weeks into the ordeal, she began to flutter her eyelashes and make what appeared to be purposeful movements. We were amazed and cautiously hopeful that perhaps her mom was right. I left for the day and began my hour-long drive home. Halfway home I realized that there was still a "do not resuscitate" order on the chart. I immediately turned around and drove back to the hospital to remove the DNR order. When I returned the next morning, in report I learned that she had arrested during the night and was successfully resuscitated. The gratitude in the eyes of her mom when I came in to begin my daily care was enough satisfaction to last a lifetime and validate that I was where I needed to be in my life.

I also began to believe in miracles, because after a rather long period in rehab, my patient went back to nursing school and finished her studies.

I have since moved on in my career, through various leadership positions, to become the vice president/chief nursing officer of one of the largest hospitals in the country. I have made it my goal in life to make sure that all nurses realize how valuable they are to the lives of others, and that they will experience their own stories that sustain them and make them feel that they, too, are where they need to be in life.

There are a privileged few who can say, "I am a nurse." It's the greatest performance of my life.

Val Gokenbach

2

HEART OF A NURSE

Wheresoever you go, go with all your heart.

Confucius

The Exchange

Thy purpose firm is equal to the deed. Who does the best his circumstance allows, does well, acts nobly; angels could do no more.

Edward Young

My feet hurt and I was ready to go home. Discouragement filled me as I helplessly watched my favorite ICU patient, Mr. Nunley, slowly slipping away. His old flabby heart was failing him by the minute, and time was running out for a transplant. I gazed into the dimly lit room and said a hushed good-bye to his daughters, assuring them that I would be back tomorrow. We exchanged forced smiles of fading hope.

As I prepared to leave, my head nurse came up to me and asked if I would like to go watch a heart transplant: Mr. Nunley's! I ran back into his room to share the good news. Hope and sadness filled his eyes as I told him that I was going to another local hospital to observe the harvesting of his new heart and then come back for his transplant. I hugged his daughters and called my husband to let him know I wouldn't be coming home until late.

The organ donor was a gentleman in his thirties who wasn't wearing a helmet when his motorcycle crashed. This father of three small children was giving one last gift of life to five or six other people before the machines were turned off. I choked back tears as I pondered his wife and children. How would she tell them that Daddy would never be coming home again? I marveled at her courage to share the life of her loved one with others.

As we entered the OR, a beautiful but beastly thought kept invading my mind: *today one must die in order for another to live.*

That is when I looked up and saw her. The nurse on the other end of this story shuffled into the OR with blood-shot, tired eyes that spoke volumes. She came in and out of the operating room to provide updates to the donor's grieving family. With awkwardness, the two of us talked about the families. We each knew what our purpose was on that day. Her role was to stand in the gap for the grieving family. She took on grief and passed on hope as she hugged them. My role was to stand in the gap for Mr. Nunley's family. I passed on the joy and absorbed their guilt through my support. She left the OR quietly and respectfully once his heart was removed and placed in the cooler.

The heart was quickly escorted by ambulance to the surgical suite of Mr. Nunley. Artificial life support took over as the gray, oversized, flabby muscle was removed. I was overcome with fear and hope when, for a few minutes, his chest was completely empty. There was no turning back. Then, the new, firm, pink heart was presented and stitch by stitch it became one with Mr. Nunley's body. We all held our breath and watched the EKG monitor as a defibrillator shock started his new life. Shouts of joy and victory rang out on this side of the exchange.

I ran down the hall to the waiting room to share the news with his family. It was finished! Life prevailed even in the face of death. Tears flowed as they expressed gratitude for the donor and his family. A new life and new hope filled all of our eyes as the exchange of life was completed.

As I drove home in the dark early-morning hours, I was overcome with emotion. I thought of the widowed wife, the grieving children alone in bed, and the nurse who became a stitch in their lives on the day that their hearts broke. Because of their pain and loss, my patient would have life and joy. Then I realized my purpose as a nurse even more clearly. Nurses stand in the gap, like the heart bypass machine, in the lives of their patients. One nurse may hold the hand of death, while another holds the hand of life.

Our eyes tell their specific stories and our hugs uphold one another, and each day the exchange continues in the lives of nurses and their patients.

Cyndi S. Schatzman

Christmas in July

Children are God's apostles, sent forth, day by day, to preach of love, and hope and peace.

J. R. Lowell

A drop of sweat trickled down the side of my face. As I walked through the door into the building, a blast of cool air enveloped me.

"Thank goodness for air-conditioning!" I said loudly to the receptionist in the lobby. She nodded in agreement as she answered a call and I got onto the elevator.

"What number?" asked a little boy in a red wagon being pulled by his mom.

I looked at him and smiled. "Number five."

He pushed the button as he smiled back at me with blue eyes that sparkled. He had no hair, and his mouth was covered with a paper mask. He wasn't from my floor . . . the masks on my floor were oxygen masks, and they still had their own hair. As a pediatric nurse in a pediatric hospital these sights were a common and accepted part of my job.

It was July 24, a sweltering summer day. But when the

elevator doors opened to the fifth floor, it was like a scene from a winter wonderland. There was a lighted Christmas tree in the corner and paper snowflakes hanging from every ceiling tile. Red ribbons adorned all the doorknobs of the patient rooms, and snowmen were pasted on every other available open space. The Christmas carol "We Wish You a Merry Christmas" played in the background, harmonized by Alvin and the Chipmunks. The playroom was filled with children with oxygen tanks and IV poles in tow. There was much laughter and giggling going on as the "play lady" turned to me and said, "Merry Christmas! We are celebrating Christmas in July . . . so that makes today Christmas Eve! Hope you've got your shopping done!"

I smiled at her inventiveness and said, "What a great idea, Betsy! Two Christmases in one year. These kids must have been *really* good!"

As my afternoon shift began and I started my assignment, I saw each of Santa's "July elves" I was assigned to, all gathered in the playroom, still giggling and listening to the Chipmunks. I did a quick check to make sure everyone was okay, and let them get back to the fun.

After playtime was finished and IV poles and oxygen tanks with kids attached were returned to their rooms, I began my rounds.

I saved Stacey for last so I could spend more time with her as needed. She was waiting for me, with that slightly lopsided grin and those huge brown eyes. I had been caring for her for many months.

Her voice sounded far away with the oxygen mask pulled tightly over her cheeks. "Kathy, what do you like best about Christmas?"

I didn't really think about my answer, I just said, "I love decorating the tree. I have some special ornaments that remind me of people I love."

While doing her treatments we talked about Christmas,

and I told her part of a story I remembered from when I was her age, about a mouse that ate Santa's cake. I couldn't remember the end and what happened to the mouse, but I said I would try to find out.

I could see she was really tired when her treatment to clear her lungs was finished. She fell asleep during dinner while watching TV; she didn't have the energy of most other eight-year-olds. I was conscious of the subtle changes, and I knew her treatment options were limited. I understood that she was slipping away. No matter how much I loved her, I could not change that.

Stacey slept much of the evening. As usual, she awakened when I came to say goodnight. It was a ritual we had started when I first started caring for her. Whenever my shift was almost over, I would come to tell her a story, she would brush her teeth and say her prayers, and I would hug and kiss her and tuck her in her bed for the night.

Since it was Christmas Eve in July, I recited "The Night Before Christmas" for her. Just as I was about to leave, she handed me a small package wrapped in white tissue paper and tied with a red ribbon. I was touched and surprised. "Can I open it now since it is after midnight and it is Christmas . . . in July?"

"No, I want you to wait for the real Christmas, with snow, and trees, and Santa . . . in December."

I gave her another gentle squeeze, and said, "You are so special to me. I love you. I can't wait till Christmas to see what it is!"

She smiled from beneath her oxygen mask and said, "You have to promise you will wait."

I assured her I would wait, just as she asked.

The dog days of summer turned into the cool, crisp days of fall. Stacey and I watched from her hospital room as the children played in the park across the street. Soon the brilliant crimson and yellow of the leaves heralded the arrival of October. Stacey's breathing was becoming increasingly difficult and she required more oxygen to keep her comfortable. Her usually sallow complexion was now a bluish hue, and she chose her words carefully whenever she spoke. It required most of her energy to talk, and when she said, "I'm tired," it wasn't just tired. She was tired of fighting for every breath.

Stacey wrote a note to me that afternoon to ask if I would "Pleeeese find out what happened to that mouse that ate Santa's cake. I want to know how the story ends."

I had forgotten about telling her that tale until she reminded me about our Christmas in July party. The next morning before work, I called the family friend who had told me the story when I was young. I told him the circumstances and all about Stacey, and that she was waiting for the end of the story. He gladly told the story again, and this time, I wrote it down.

During Stacey's treatment the next afternoon, I recited the rest of the tale about the mouse that ate Santa's cake. She smiled when I finished, and with great effort said, "Thank you. Now I know what happens at the end."

When her grandmother arrived that evening, as the sunset glowed pink and purple in the sky, Stacey closed her eyes and died peacefully in her grandma's arms.

Now her story was completed too.

I was with her when she died, as I had been on many afternoons and evenings of her young life. I missed her terribly. I missed her big brown eyes and her lopsided smile that drew me eagerly back to work every day. I missed the faraway sound of her voice behind her oxygen mask, and the hugs and kisses she gave me at the beginning and end of my workdays on my first job as a pediatric nurse. I felt her absence every day from that day on.

But time passed, as it does. We celebrated Thanksgiving

with a feast together at work, and the holiday rush began. Soon it was the real Christmas Eve.

I returned home from work that evening and as the clock struck midnight, I took out the package Stacey had given me in July. On the tag in her childish scrawl, she'd written, "To Kathy. I love you. Do not open until December 25." I slowly unwound the red ribbon and removed the crinkled tissue paper. Inside the package was a white snowman with big green polka dots. He wore a black felt hat, had blue button eyes, and a red, lopsided grin. A loop of green yarn wrapped as a scarf around his neck, and another loop was glued to his back so he was ready to hang on the tree. As my tears fell on the snowman, I recalled the words I said to her when she asked what I liked best about Christmas . . . decorating the tree with special ornaments that remind me of people I love.

Each Christmas as I unwrap the ornament, the tissue paper becomes more fragile and yellowed with age. I reread Stacey's simple declaration of love and caress the polka-dot snowman. His lopsided grin is a legacy of the little girl that I loved.

Kathleen E. Jones

Sacred Moments

Ritual is the way you carry the presence of the sacred. Ritual is the spark that must not go out.

Christina Baldwin

It was a typical day in the emergency department—busy. We are always busy; in fact, we are the busiest ED in the state. I was assigned the float position, meaning it was my job to circulate and help nurses assigned to specific stations when needed.

A call came over the radio from emergency medical services saying they were bringing in a nine-week-old female baby in respiratory arrest. The nurse working the trauma assignment received the infant. Tragically, in spite of every effort possible, the baby did not survive.

Not long after, the ED nurse liaison approached me. One of her many jobs was to care for the families of loved ones in critical situations. "I heard you have some experience in art. Do you know anything about casting in plaster?"

I told her I did. She handed me the materials she had gathered and instructed me to go to the trauma room and make a cast of the infant's foot for the family.

I entered the room and instantly felt palpable grief. Dad and Mom stood over the gurney staring at a tiny bundle wrapped in blankets. Grandma was holding their other child, who appeared to be around two years old. They barely spoke and when they did, it was in hushed tones. Everyone seemed stunned, unable to move, not sure of their next step.

I quietly introduced myself and said I had come to help make foot imprints of their baby girl. They all stared at me, eyes red and glazed. I looked at Dad and figured he would be best to invest in the mechanical part of our project. I quickly got him involved in mixing the plaster material and putting it into the molds. He seemed grateful for something to do at a time when he couldn't possibly know what to do next. His voice, hushed at first, became fuller.

"Press her little hand here," I said softly as we made impressions, first of her hands, then of her feet.

It was time to get the women involved. "Here are buttons, bows, glitter, beads, and other decorations for the molds."

They began to pick through these items, each making suggestions, discussing how to decorate the molded impressions. Their voices became stronger as they focused on the project at hand. I stood back watching them and realized the energy of the room had changed from grief and despair to focused creativity.

As they completed their creation, they began to talk about what they should do next, who they would call, where they would go. They stared at the molds, eyes gleaming, each understanding they had created a treasure that would always be cherished: the remembrance of a life lived, too short but so very sweet.

One after another, they gathered their things. Slowly, each held the precious baby girl one last time, softly saying their good-byes to their beloved bundled in a blanket.

Then Dad handed her to me.

Mom was the last one to exit. She turned with a hint of a smile and mouthed, "Thank you."

I held her child; she held their treasured creation.

One of the tasks we nurses are called to do is to assist in the death process. What happened in those shared moments with that young family was something much deeper and richer . . . a sacred ritual in nursing.

Jude L. Fleming

Nurse, Heal Thyself

Her ways are ways of pleasantness, and all her paths are peace.

Proverbs 3:17

I recognized the legal-sized envelope resting inside my mailbox: my nursing license renewal form. Two years before I had filled out the paperwork to renew my license, hopeful I could resume my career, despite my obvious injuries. It was a hope I had clung to for ten years.

I'd been an impossibly naive young woman, ready to save my little piece of the world at my new job at a downtown Atlanta hospital. With my crisply ironed nursing whites and my freshly printed diploma, I felt ready to fulfill the plans God had laid out for my life.

The post-op patient in bed 419 didn't mean to hurt me. Although we were not a surgical floor, the man had been assigned to a room at the end of my hall as a favor to one of the doctors on staff. No one expected him to have a drug-induced psychotic episode, least of all a novice nurse like me. With an unnatural scream, he kicked me into the

wall. The blow seared a trail of unbelievable pain across my
buttocks and down my right leg, ending behind my knee.
My toes and the bottom of my foot went numb and cold.

Like a dutiful nurse, I continued working throughout
the rest of the night, dragging my right foot a bit as I dis-
pensed medication and attended patients for surgery.
Only morning and a visit to the emergency room would
reveal the force of the attack on my body. A series of discs
in my lower back had been ruptured, putting pressure on
my sciatic nerve. The doctors reacted conservatively,
treating me with rest, drugs, and traction, but soon it
became apparent that surgery was my only option.

No one ever sat me down and told me about the possible
long-term effects of my injuries and, to be honest, I never
considered it. I naively thought I would have the affected
discs repaired, recuperate for a couple of months, then get on
with my life. It wasn't until the day after my surgery, while I
drifted in and out of sleep, that I heard a conversation
between my husband, Dan, and my neurosurgeon. Profound
nerve damage. Chronic pain with periods of paralysis.

"She'll never be able to work as a nurse again."

Even in my semiconscious state, my heart shattered.
Me, not be a nurse? I couldn't fathom the idea. I wanted to
scream, but couldn't find my voice.

Slowly, I started to heal. And as my body began to
return to normal, so did my will. I decided not to take the
doctor's prognosis lying down. I would fight for my career.

Physical therapy appointments, insurance negotiations,
and depression filled my first few weeks post-op. I
stopped eating and lost so much weight the visiting nurse
thought I had an eating disorder. The arguments began
between the hospital and my doctors as to what kind of
work I would physically be able to do. Eventually, the hospital and I parted ways.

I started searching the want ads, but each interview

ended in disappointment. No one would hire an inexperienced nurse with my medical history. Some of my friends suggested I keep my back problems a secret, but I couldn't do that and live with myself.

At twenty-three, I found myself unemployable.

But I refused to give up. Six months and hundreds of résumés later, a research facility offered me a position. For the next six years, I worked in pediatric research, teaching parents how to care for their high-risk infants. I was finally doing the work God had called me to do.

Yet, physically, I wasn't doing so well. I tried to pretend everything was okay, laughing over the times I'd trip over my numb foot or ignoring the pain running across my hip and down my leg. When I began to fall on a consistent basis, I contacted my doctor.

An alphabet of tests followed—MRIs, EMGs, CAT scans. Weeks later, the doctor had a verdict: stenosis of the spinal column, extensive nerve damage, more ruptured discs. My nursing career was officially over.

My body understood the truth, but my heart rebelled. Nursing defined me as a person, defined the faith I had in God's plan for my life. If my career was gone, who was I? What was I going to do with the rest of my life?

I was ashamed of my disability, believing it made me less of a person. In my anger, I backed away from my husband, daughters, and friends. I thought I was doing them a favor. After all, why would they want to have anything to do with a twenty-nine-year-old cripple? Our home became a battlefield as I slipped further into depression. One evening, Dan came home to his packed clothes and my demand that he leave.

My world imploded.

"Please get some help," my parents begged. I agreed to meet with a counselor who helped me face the anger that had been brewing inside of me since the attack. I finally asked the question that had plagued me since the moment my patient had slammed me against the wall. Why had God allowed this to happen to me?

Her answer? "Why not?"

She told me the story of Paul, a man who had seen his life change on the road to Damascus. He too had a disability, a thorn of the flesh that he asked the Lord to take from him. Paul never found relief from his physical suffering but that didn't stop him from living a worthwhile life.

I had a choice. I could live my life sitting at home, pain and anger my constant companions. Or I could get involved with the world around me, starting with my husband and girls. Would the pain go away? No, but the worthlessness of my existence would cease.

Within a week, I reconciled with Dan. I started slowly, volunteering in my daughter's classroom. My involvement soon blossomed into teaching mentally disabled children. Our family went back to church, where I found new joy in singing with the choir. The angry wrinkles that slashed my face slowly faded into smile lines. Although the physical pain never went away, I found a life worth living.

Nursing still plays a part in my life. The skills I learned helped me to care for my dying grandfather. And my father swears he is still around because I forced him to recognize the symptoms of a heart attack.

Though nursing no longer defines who I am, as I sorted the mail, I knew I had a choice.

I tossed the envelope aside, unopened. I knew I didn't need paperwork to do His will. License or no, in my caring heart, I am still a nurse.

Patty Smith Hall

A Nurse's Touch

And in the sweetness of friendship let there be laughter and the sharing of pleasures. For in the dew of little things the heart finds its morning and is refreshed.

Kahlil Gibran

In my perpetual haste I rushed by the building but failed to notice moisture pooled beneath a rainspout. A transparent film of ice floated on top.

My clumsy fall required a metal plate and screws to line up my broken bones to heal. The doctor called it a "tib fib double reduction."

I called it excruciating.

He explained that both the tibia and fibula were broken. I literally didn't have that leg to stand on!

"Aggressive physical therapy will enable you to walk with only a slight limp. But you'll have to give up those high heels."

When I tried to stand, I simply fainted. My optimism

faded a bit more each time I slumped, and my recuperation required someone to stay nearby.

Friends and family rearranged busy lives. Soon a Maryjo-sitting and meal delivery schedule hung on the refrigerator. Meals came in. Dirty laundry went out. Freshly folded clothes came back. One sweet soul made my floors and oven sparkle.

These activities underscored my incapacity. I was a doer unaccustomed to sitting still. The vulnerability I felt was overwhelming.

I didn't want to see anyone. I didn't want to talk to anyone. I didn't even want to read. I lay in a medicated haze of pain and self-pity when Trish entered quietly. She juggled family and her career more deftly than most, but I hadn't expected to see her here. Not with her shift work and tight schedule.

"I felt so bad for you when I heard about this. I know how hard it must be for you, being forced to slow down. And the pain from that kind of injury is pretty tough."

She softly closed the bedroom door, turned down the lights, and began arranging pillows and bedcovers with practiced dexterity.

"This is quite a trauma. Try to be patient. You have to be open to the healing process. Rest. And take the pain medications as directed. Muscling your way through and doing without only makes things worse. You'll only be on these meds for a short time."

I had to listen to this longtime friend. I'd watched Trish go back to school when our sons were still quite young, and I'd always admired the tenacity it took to complete her nursing degree.

Still, the truth she spoke I found hard to take, and my protests and resentment popped out despite my efforts to stifle them.

"Look at me. Other people are running Mom's taxi,

doing my wash, cooking meals . . . even cleaning my oven, for heaven's sake. I can't even go to the bathroom by myself without blacking out!"

"Feels weird for you to be on the accepting end of things, doesn't it? You'll get used to it. Healing doesn't take forever. Now, accept one more thing," she said softly.

"Allow me to give you a sponge bath. My patients tell me I'm pretty good at them."

Trish and I had been friends over a decade. We'd taken care of sick children, shared recipes and outings. But . . . give me a bath? I was feverish and sweaty. Worse, my own perspiration, tinged acrid by medication, smelled foreign and awful.

No way. Embarrassed, I shook my head.

"You'll feel refreshed, more like yourself."

She turned and started wetting a cloth in the steaming pan of water I had not seen until that moment. She held up a bottle of baby lotion, the thick pink kind.

"If you use this instead of soap, there's no need to rinse. It moisturizes your skin and smells fresh."

She placed the now-saturated cloth beneath my nose. The light aroma was very pleasing. Just the thought of smelling like that made me nod "Okay."

With gentle strength she positioned each limb so that she did all the work, my modesty intact. All I had to do was relax. She swirled the warm cloth in each crease and crevice, wiping away misery with the dead skin cells. She carefully lifted limb after limb. Fingers and toes received attention, and as she lotioned each digit, encouragement soaked in.

Then she shampooed my hair, firm fingers massaging my crusty scalp. My matted hair curled again. I'll never know how she did it without sloshing water everywhere.

Trish's sponge bath gave me so much more than the refreshment of a clean body. She restored my dignity and

gave me a calm that saw me through the many tough days
of healing ahead.

My dear friend had a nurse's touch that was the best
medicine for my aching soul.

Maryjo Faith Morgan

Finding Christ in a Hospice

Assuredly I say to you, unless you are converted and become little children, you will by no means enter the kingdom of heaven.

Matthew 18:3

Hospice is a place where terminally ill patients go, not just to die, but to live out their lives in peace, comfort, and dignity. One wealthy young lady was admitted; she was very beautiful, except the lower half of her jaw was deteriorated by the advance of the cancerous disease. For the first three months, she was very bitter, sarcastic, nasty, and abusive to the staff and all the other residents.

One day, a young LPN took the time to put some makeup on the woman's eyes and cheeks. Then she wrapped a scarf around the woman's lower face and led her outside where she could sit on a park bench and enjoy the warm spring sun.

Across the street, some young boys were playing baseball on a makeshift diamond. Sure enough, one of the older boys hit a foul ball and it rolled across the street and stopped at the feet of the lady sitting on the bench. A small boy, about eight years old, sauntered across the street to retrieve the ball. He picked up the ball and tossed it back across the street. Then the boy stopped and looked at the young woman for a long time. Suddenly he climbed up on the bench, hugged her, and kissed her on the forehead. "You are a very beautiful lady," said the boy. He got down and ran back to the game.

A miraculous thing happened at that moment. All the anger and bitterness seemed to flow out of the young woman. She went back into that hospice and began to help others. With her wealth, she provided makeup and wigs for the other women and even personally helped them improve their appearances as best they could in their last days. She was a source of encouragement and joy to both staff and all the residents—the first one to share a tear, give a hug, or hold those in agony and fear.

All this happened because an LPN and a small boy became Christ to the lady when she needed it the most. This enabled her to become Christ to others.

Father Gent Ullrich
as told to John Fagley

Halloween

Laughter is the sun that drives winter from the human face.

Victor Hugo

It was almost Halloween and I didn't know what to wear. I had been working at Emanuel Rehabilitation Center for several years and always managed to come up with a clever costume, so now it was expected of me. Last year, I went as a member of the "backup team" and wore my son's dress clothes backward, with a mask of a handsome man on the back of my head. I got a lot of laughs walking down the hall.

I pondered what costume would again cheer up the quadriplegics I had been caring for.

Tom, a good-looking twenty-four-year-old quad, was constantly yelling, "Jean, come here. Please rub my nose. Jean, scratch my head. Jean, dial the phone for me."

Then Mary, across the hall, joined him with her demands. They knew they were not supposed to yell "Jean" when they needed help, but were to bump the paddle on either side of their head to turn on the call light. But calling out my name expressed their urgency and got quicker results. So they called and called and called. That's when I had a great idea: I'd dress up as a call girl!

From the drawerful of my daughter's discarded dance costumes, I retrieved some sheer burgundy tights and covered them with black fishnet stockings. I donned a slinky burgundy top, then, over that went a pink, loosely crocheted dress that came to midthigh, covered by a short, pink, see-through, sheer skirt. My husband, Al, thought I looked quite authentic and gorgeous with my reddish-brown wig and fake leopard jacket. Across my chest, I fastened a big sign: YOU CALLED?

"This ought to make even Grumpy Bob chuckle," I said, imagining the old quadriplegic man who had been so depressed. I inspected my reflection in front of my full-length bedroom mirror. "Hmm, not bad," I teased my husband. "Maybe I shouldn't have become a nurse. If only I were thirty-some years younger . . . " I shimmied around in front of the mirror, my dangling earrings bouncing and the sheer skirt swishing.

When I arrived at work at 3:00 PM the Halloween party was in progress. Everyone howled with laughter when I arrived. The wheelchair salesman greeted me with open arms.

The social worker said, "This wouldn't be so funny if you weren't so out of character."

"I'm glad you said that," I said. "This reception is more than I was mentally prepared for."

"Jean! Jean!" I heard Tom's familiar call.

"Jean!" Mary echoed.

With a sigh and a smile I slithered into Tom's room first, smacking my gum. "You called?"

He burst out laughing.

"You gave me the idea to be a call girl since you know

you're always calling my name," I said.

He laughed harder than I had ever heard him laugh, probably harder than he had since his accident. "I can't believe I have a call girl for my nurse!"

Patients laughed all evening as I went around answering lights and doing care. An old male stroke patient who couldn't talk flashed a crooked smile and I noted a glint in his twinkling eyes. Even Grumpy Bob laughed each time I saw him. "Jean, you're really something!" Seeing him so jovial made the whole thing worthwhile.

Every Halloween after that, someone would beg me to wear that costume again, but once was enough.

When I retired in 1994, one nurse said, "Jean, don't you still want to work 'on call'?"

Jean Kirnak

Miss Benjamin

Gratitude is the memory of the heart.

Italian Proverb

My sleep was fitful, punctuated with the hospital sounds of muffled conversations and carts squeaking down the hall. It was almost morning. In my drowsiness, the unwelcome thoughts returned again . . . *I don't want to die! I'm only sixteen! I long for proms, and boyfriends, and . . . life!*

A week before my doctor had discovered another large tumor in my head. I was snatched by my parents and driven to specialists at a university hospital in Michigan, over a thousand miles from my home in Florida. The experts ordered medical tests to help them determine how to save my life. Could they?

I didn't hear the door to my hospital room open, but in the darkness I sensed a presence at my bedside. When she spoke, her voice was as sweet as slow, dark molasses.

"Sorry to wake you so early, sugar, but I need to take your temperature," she announced, as she stuck a cold thermometer under my tongue. Then, with a touch as smooth as black velvet, she found the pulse in my pale wrist. When I peered up at her, the white nurse's uniform was a stark contrast to the dark skin of the pretty woman standing next to my bed.

"What's your name?" I asked sleepily.

"Miss Benjamin."

It was the early 1960s and I lived in the South. I didn't know many African Americans, but I instantly bonded with Miss Benjamin.

My parents rented a room from a family across the street from the hospital and befriended them. They had a son in his late teens named Don. He and his friend Tommy, worked at the hospital. Many early mornings they came before visiting hours to see me. Miss Benjamin cooperated with their illegal intrusions and allowed them to stay and lift my spirits.

After the doctors conferred, the news was grim. The massive tumor between my brain and my eyes would be removed immediately, but the risky operation could leave me blind. I felt there was little hope.

"The good Lord is going to take care of you," Miss Benjamin assured me the morning of my surgery. Then her soft voice promised, "I'm scheduled to have the afternoon off, but I'm going to stay on duty and look after you." Knowing she would be there eased my fear.

I survived the surgery and was relieved to see Miss Benjamin when I woke up. Yes, I could *see* her!

But the days of recovery were brutal. My face was wrapped in a beehive of gauze. The pain was intense when Miss Benjamin carefully changed the bandages. I felt scarred and ugly. I didn't want the boys to see me. "Tell them not to come in," I cried.

Early one morning I thought I heard pebbles hit my window.

"What's that noise?" Miss Benjamin asked as she breezed through the door with a thermometer in her hand. Then she walked to the window, golden with dawn.

"Lord have mercy! I think you have visitors! Let me help you walk over here!"

I could see two heads poking over the edge of the roof a few feet above my window. Don and Tommy found a way to visit me, without making me self-conscious about my bandages. We talked, between the rooftop and the open window, that day and many more.

Miss Benjamin was a real sport about our teenage antics and she supported our clandestine encounters. Each morning, she walked me to the window, tugged it open, then tiptoed back as I greeted my friends. My hospital confinement was often excruciating, but the rooftop visits took my mind off my recovery and made my days exciting.

On the morning I was to be dismissed from the hospital and head home to Florida, I awoke early to the sound of pebbles hitting glass. I leaned out over the windowsill and looked up at the two handsome smiles beaming down from the roof. Miss Benjamin came into the room and put her arm around me. It would be the last time my special nurse and the two boys crouched on the roof would be part of my life

"Since you're checking out today," Tommy announced with a twinkle in his eye, "Don and I made something for you. Something that will remind you about what you loved most here."

My two faithful visitors carefully lowered their gift.

I stared in disbelief at the papier-mâché likeness the boys had crafted. The face was brown with beautiful, gentle features. A black wig adorned the top of the head.

"We know how much you love Miss Benjamin," Don called down from the rooftop. "Now she will always be with you."

And she is.

Miriam Hill

The Day "Doc" Goss Became a Nurse

*One of the things that has helped me as much
as any other, is not how long I am going to live,
but how much I can do while living.*

George Washington Carver

In March 1969, shortly after graduating from the United
States Navy's corpsman school, Jim Goss received his
orders to report to Alpha Company, First Battalion 7th
Marine Regiment of the First Marine Division.

Jim became a navy sailor attached to the Fleet Marine
Force. Normally this would be a nightmare, given the 200
years of rivalry between these two services, but Jim was a
corpsman and they were special. Upon arriving in
Vietnam, marine green was the color for all. The young
marines, as well as the older noncoms and officers, were
now "his boys" in the field and he was "Doc."

Jim's nineteen weeks in corpsman school, however,
could not have prepared him for the carnage that awaited
him in Southeast Asia's jungles. He witnessed and treated
wounds that experienced emergency room physicians in

this country never dreamed of seeing. And he treated those men while under fire.

In late 1969, North Vietnamese regulars overran the firebase where Jim was just outside of Da Nang. During that firefight, Jim held compresses with one hand and his .45 automatic pistol with the other. He covered wounded bodies with his own trying to keep them alive. With adrenaline running through his veins, Jim did not know how bad the shrapnel from an RPG (rocket-propelled grenade) had wounded him until hours later when he took a shower.

For his valor, Jim Goss received the Bronze Star, and for his wounds he received the Purple Heart. And from his "boys" he received their undying love and thanks.

When Jim returned home from his military service he went to work as a parts manager at an automobile dealership for five years. But his passion for caring called him and he went to nursing school and graduated with an associate degree. "Doc" Goss had become a nurse. He worked in the emergency rooms of several hospitals and also managed a paramedic unit.

Then his passion for caring called him further—full circle. He went to work for the U.S. Veterans Hospital in Coatsville, Pennsylvania, working in the post-traumatic stress disorder unit that he heads today.

He eventually earned a bachelor of science degree in nursing, but nothing has really changed with Jim as he takes care of "his boys."

Though he is their charge nurse, they still call him "Doc."

Patrick Mendoza

Goodnight, Harry

Therefore, comfort each other and edify one another, just as you are doing.

1 Thessalonians 5:11

My name is Harry. When I was forty-two, I was dynamic and distinguished, independent in life as I worked or traveled. Travel was my passion. By the time I was forty-five, I looked sixty. And now, at age forty-seven, I look ninety.

What robbed me of vitality, dignity, and very life was AIDS and several of its henchmen—the worst of which is an aggressive cancerlike disease named Kaposi's sarcoma.

My travels are now limited to being rolled on my side, and back to the other side, while lying in bed in an inpatient hospice. I have come here to die and will oblige fate by doing so.

Kind, gentle hands care for me, but unfortunately their kindness cannot stop the pain of wood-hard legs, rotting from within from the sarcoma. Being turned is now a major agony, even with the narcotics I'm given.

Often I am uncertain of who is caring for me, even though through the medicinal haze the voices are familiar and sometimes I can connect them fleetingly to a name of a friend or a nurse or an aide. Two weeks ago, I joked with them all.

Now I would trade my life for a moment of laughter and relief.

"Harry. Harry. How are you tonight?"

I recognize the voice as that of a woman who works the evening shift, although I could not have told you until a second ago if it was day or night. Her name comes and goes with an ebb and surge of pain.

I try to respond to her question, but all that I can manage is a low sound. I am not sure myself if it is the greeting I meant to say, or a low moan. Even though it is of my creation, I do not recognize the sound.

I know she is going to pat me on my shoulder, like always. And she does. And I smile what must be an internal smile.

I can hear the stretching of latex as she gloves her hands and the low click of the pump that pushes steady but now not-so-small doses of morphine into my welcoming veins. I can feel the pressure of her fingers as she checks the IV site in my right arm, and all the while she talks to me softly.

Suddenly what attention I can muster is filled with the image of fruit, the smell of fruit; probably her scented shampoo because they discourage perfume here. The smell of berries is subtle, distant, yet pleasing, comforting.

There is a pause. I know she is clasping the head of the stethoscope in her hand to warm it. I know this because she always does this. She is both methodical and kind. It comforts me and I begin to drift.

Then an almost shocking damp coolness is against my face. I turn my head away because of the surprise of the sensation. I should have remembered. She always gently wipes my face with a cool washcloth. How could I forget something that feels so good?

The changing of the bandages on my legs is the opposite. It sends pain shooting up my calves, thighs, and throughout my body. No amount of morphine helps. No amount of gentleness helps. It is always an agony. I am sure it is horrible for her, too, because there are times when I can smell the rotting flesh. Still, she performs this mutually horrible task, not because she is paid to, but because she cares.

I can hear the sounds of instruments being placed in a tray, plastic bags opened and tied shut, and all the while she continues to talk softly. I am not lucid enough to understand all that she says, but the words and her tone comfort me as the intense pain from my legs subsides slightly.

There is another snap of latex and the running of water as she washes her hands across the room. And then, once again, a calm, quiet, reassuring voice comes to me above the dullness of my senses.

"Goodnight, Harry." I feel a pat on the shoulder and the softest of kisses on my forehead. I try to discern which side of life and death derived that kiss. There is an angel there. I know.

Harry J. as told to Daniel James

Comforter

Of one thing I am certain, the body is not the measure of healing—peace is the measure.

George Melton

"My baby, I want my baby!" I sobbed when my first pregnancy ended at thirteen weeks in a miscarriage. Numbly, I'd nodded while my doctor scheduled a D&C surgery. My husband's worried eyes were the last thing I saw before the anesthesia took effect and swept me into a dreamless sleep.

As I woke from my drugged-induced slumber, I felt the finality of my loss. I cried for the child who was so wanted, yet inexplicably gone.

I felt soft tissues dab my cheeks as someone gently dried my tears.

"I want my baby," I whispered.

"Oh Cindy, I know you do," a kind voice murmured.

It was a nurse in the post-op room. I couldn't see her clearly without my glasses and through my tears. But I thought she must be beautiful because she didn't *shush* me, she just kept mopping my tears. The anesthetic numbed my body, yet left my emotions raw, and I was unable to suppress the grief that seemed to swell from my empty womb.

When my sobs subsided the nurse leaned down very close to me and said, "Cindy, I lost my husband three months ago, and he loved babies. I know that he has welcomed your child in heaven and I know that he'll watch over him."

My eyes cleared and I saw that she was young—just a few years older than me, in fact.

Her words gave me much-needed peace. Soon, I was wheeled into the recovery room, and I never saw her again. But I've not forgotten her. Out of her own grief her words wove a blanket of comfort that warmed and soothed my aching soul.

That morning when my pain was most fresh and raw, she let me grieve. If I could have seen her more clearly, I think I would've seen the traces of her own tears and the mark of her own loss, so cruel and new.

Nurses are trained to heal the body, but I was blessed with one who helped heal my heart.

Cindy Hval

3

LOVE

One word frees us of all the weight and pain of life: that word is love.

Sophocles

Perfect Child

Every child born into this world is a new thought of God, an ever-fresh and radiant possibility.

Kate Douglas Wiggin

I was working in the special care nursery as night charge nurse. After I scrubbed in, I entered the unit and glanced around. There was only one new baby since yesterday—a good-sized newborn, away from the others, wrapped in a blanket that concealed half his face. The powder blue knit blanket indicated his gender. There was no name on his Isolette.

I peeked into the warmer. *What a gorgeous baby.* He had thick, wavy blond hair, and his big blue eyes followed my gaze. He seemed more alert and observant than most newborns. His eyelashes were long and expressive.

I pulled the blanket away from his face. Then I breathed deeply. *Oh no. Cleft lip.* I tilted his head back a little and peered inside his mouth. *Cleft palate, too. Poor baby. There're surgeries ahead for you.* I stroked his cheek and smiled down at him.

In the report room the day charge nurse was edgy. I could tell she had had a rough shift. She quickly updated us on the babies who were there the night before, then the blond newborn. He was born that morning to a sixteen-year-old unwed mother who was planning on an open adoption with a thirtyish professional couple. The couple had paid all her medical expenses, had even accompanied her on doctor's visits. They were selected from three couples that the teenager had interviewed. Now the adoptive parents wanted their money back. Their lawyer had pointed out that prenatally all medical tests were negative for aberrations. The ultrasound was read as normal.

"Do they realize it's just superficial?" I interjected.

"Tell me about it," the day charge nurse said tersely. "It's not the horror of some birth defects. His brain, vital organs, body, and movements are normal. He's got a dynamite personality—you can tell by those expressive eyes."

"Everybody wants the perfect child," one of my colleagues said with a sigh.

"Did the doctor tell the adoptive parents that his condition is mostly cosmetic? That after a series of operations and possibly speech therapy, that these kids are normal, and live healthy and productive lives?"

"Yes, but the couple made it clear they want a perfect child now, not later," the day charge nurse said wearily. "To them that baby is defective merchandise."

"But that's the adoptive parents' right," another colleague said. "They expected a perfect child and the perfect child was not delivered."

I groaned. "Geez. Rejected solely because of looks. What is his name?"

The day nurse looked toward me with sad eyes. "He hasn't got one. The teenager doesn't want him, never bonded during pregnancy. Poor girl actively detached knowing he was going up for adoption. Says she wishes she had aborted and saved herself and her family a lot of pain and suffering. Now her parents are trying to come up with the money to reimburse the intended adoptive parents so they won't be sued. The baby has no one. To me, he looks like a Scotty."

That was good enough for me. I wrote down his name. "What about the other two couples?"

"They will be visiting tomorrow," the charge nurse said. "But the doctor reported that neither couple is keen on a special needs child."

I shook my head. "Hardly a special needs. Surgeons are so good at it now that a cosmetic repair is barely noticeable."

Even though Scotty had a healthy appetite and tried his hardest to suck on a specially designed nipple, he failed. Sloppy sucking left him vulnerable to pulmonary aspiration and choking, so he had to be gavage-fed. A thin flexible tube was placed from mouth to stomach, for formula feedings.

Day two of life, Scotty was moved to a crib. He was also rejected by a second couple. Twenty-four hours later, the third couple decided against adopting Scotty, too.

The day charge nurse purchased a front-pack infant carrier and we carried and cuddled Scotty during rounds. Though his time with us would be short, we wanted to convey to this tiny spirit that not everyone rejected him.

On day three of his life, his teenage birth mother went home. The next day, Scotty would be going to a foster home. A plastic surgeon visited and suggested that Scotty's lip be closed in a month or so, when he reached ten pounds. The palate would be fused later, between eighteen and thirty-six months of age. He asked if Scotty had become a ward of the state, and who he should bill for the surgeries.

"I don't know," I said, hugging Scotty against my chest. Then I prayed for this little bundle from God.

About midnight on day three, as I was gavage-feeding a growing preemie, I heard someone scrubbing in at the sink near the nursery entrance. I turned to see a nurse in a white uniform slipping on a protective gown over her clothes. She didn't look familiar.

"Can I help you?" I asked. No outside personnel are allowed in the nursery without permission or notice—any nurse knows that. I was on heightened alert.

"I'm looking for—oh there he is!" she said, walking straight over to Scotty's crib. She picked him up, kissed him on the forehead, and cradled him in her arms. "Here's my boy. I have been waiting so long for you!"

"I'm sorry," I began, "but I haven't been given notice of you coming. I'll have to call security . . . "

"Please don't," she said with a nasal tone to her voice. Then she looked up at me and smiled a crooked smile. I immediately saw the telltale marks of restorative surgery for cleft lip. The tone of her speech suggested cleft palate repair as well. "You see, I dreamed of a blond son with beautiful blue eyes and clefts . . . but my girl and boy were born normal."

"How did you know about Scotty?" I asked.

"The whole hospital knows about Scotty," she said softly. "After I heard yesterday, I went home and had the same dream again. Then, I talked to my husband and he agreed for me to visit. Now that I hold him, I know—we're going to adopt Scotty. And I think we'll keep his name. "

I washed my hands in silence.

"Is he able to suck from a bottle?"

I shook my head.

"That's okay," the nurse said, her eyes fixed on Scotty's. "My whole family knows how to gavage. My mom, your grandma, did it to me for months. Just wait until she sees you!" she told him.

Then she looked at her watch. "Oh, I have to get back to the ICU. I'll be back at the end of the shift. I'll talk to the day charge nurse and get my husband and lawyer in here. I'm so excited! Molly and Paul will be thrilled to have a baby brother."

I watched as she kissed Scotty once more and then gently placed him back in the crib. She pulled off her protective gown and headed to the nursery door. "God sent him to me," she said with a beaming smile.

"Yes," I said softly in agreement. "And He sent you for Scotty."

A perfect child for the perfect mother.

Diana M. Amadeo

Child's Therapy

Behold, children are a heritage from the Lord.

Psalm 127:3

Beth holds the door open for her five-year-old daughter, Haley, so she can maneuver her tiny red walker into the brightly decorated lobby of the children's clinic. It is a place far too familiar to Haley. She is well known to the staff. Today is a good day for Haley. Her energy level is uncharacteristically high, as she grips the handles of the walker with her small hands and guides its tiny wheels in the direction of the waiting room. Care Bears dance on her bright pink sweatsuit and blond curls bounce around her shoulders. Her twinkling blue eyes complement the big smile that is on her face.

While her mommy signs her in at the desk, Haley, ever the independent one, looks over the group of children and adults in the room. In a corner a young boy about twelve sits alone, head down, face obscured by his dark blue baseball cap. Haley slowly approaches him. Beth follows her and takes a seat nearby on a couch next to a woman who turns out to be the boy's mother.

The child's name is Timmy and his mom and Beth watch as Haley moves closer to him, trying to get his attention. Soon she stands near his chair, smiling at him even as he continues to ignore her. The other children are laughing and playing across the room in the play area, their parents appearing to be unaware of the disfigured boy and the crippled girl. Timmy's mom tells Beth that he was tragically burned over two years ago when he tried to fill a cigarette lighter with fluid, thinking he was helping his dad. He did not realize he had spilled some of the fluid onto his pajamas and when he flicked the lighter to see if it worked, the pj's caught on fire. Since that time, the once outgoing, happy little boy had become withdrawn and keenly aware of his disfigurement. There was much scarring on his neck and hands. He always wore the cap to try to hide the ugly, bright pink ridges climbing up to his face, and he wore long-sleeved clothing to cover his rough, scarred hands.

While listening to the story, Beth notices Haley still standing closely, almost protectively, by Timmy, who is now glancing at her from underneath the bill of his cap. Just then, Nurse Anne, Haley's favorite, walks through the room and calls out Haley's name. Haley reluctantly moves away from the corner while looking back at Timmy. It is as though she can sense his pain. Anne quietly observes this and reaches out her arms to Haley with tears in her eyes. She lifts the little girl from her walker and Haley snuggles her head on Anne's shoulder as she's carried into the exam room.

Timmy's mother explains how Anne has tried everything to reach her son, but in spite of her persistent, loving efforts, he rejects her and everyone else there.

A short while later, Haley and her mom are preparing to leave the clinic and head for the promised visit to the ice cream parlor. Beth turns to the exit door, but Haley is whispering to Anne, who is kneeling face-to-face with her. The two conspirators, the endearing disabled child and the caring nurse, smile at one another, hug, and then part.

"Just a minute, Mommy," Haley says.

She crosses the room to where Timmy still sits in his solitary corner. She puts her tiny fingers on his tightly closed fist almost hidden in his jacket sleeve. He lifts his eyes to meet hers and does not pull away.

Haley whispers, "I think you are beautiful."

Tears appear in Timmy's eyes as Haley continues, "Every night my mommy prays with me and we ask God to take care of me. Tonight we will pray for you."

The adults in the room who had previously avoided looking at Timmy are now watching and listening. Timmy looks directly at Haley, then holds his arms out to her. She leans away from the safety of her walker and into his embrace.

Barbara Haile

A Sign of Love

The greatest pleasure of life is love.

Sir William Temple

Wandering down the halls of the locked unit of a long-term care facility, you will see many things. People look lost and lonely; they smile at you as if you were family and they walk aimlessly throughout the building, which is both familiar yet strange to them. Today is in a previous time—the year is 1936, when the war just broke out, or 1952, when they gave birth to their first child.

Working in the nursing home you become the residents' family. In you they see their daughter or son, the one who never visits, and they feel comfortable and happy knowing that someone who cares about them is close by.

Language is lost for them. There are no more utterances of, "I love you," no more "hellos"—it's just the silent sound of people who are trapped inside themselves, trapped by a disease called Alzheimer's.

As a recreation therapist it has been my job to cultivate the incredible creative spirit that lies within these people and provide them a way of having fun and expressing themselves—with or without words.

This is where our story begins.

It was an early morning as I walked around the locked unit. I gave Sheila her good morning kiss and Shirley a hug as we usually did every morning.

The unit was quiet except for the familiar tapping noise. I went into one of the small living rooms to discover Marion tapping the top of her chair. This was a daily occurrence. We knew she was trying to tell us something because she only tapped when she wanted our attention.

I walked over to her and kneeled on the floor beside her. She looked at me with grandmotherly eyes, pursed her lips, and gave me a kiss. Then pointing to me, she tapped on her armchair and smiled.

This event went on every day. I always gave her a kiss and sat with her, as Marion didn't utter a word. I could tell by her eyes she desperately wanted to tell me something; I just couldn't figure out what it was.

One day the tapping on her chair was uncontrollable. Every tactic to distract and redirect her was tried, yet nothing seemed to work. I was downstairs doing paper-work when I heard my name on the PA system instructing me to come right away.

I dashed to the elevator thinking something was cata-strophically wrong. Did someone fall? Had someone died? My heart pounded. I found the nurse in charge of the unit frantically trying to deal with Marion, who was now very upset and shaking.

I went to her, smiled, put my hand over the hand that was tapping and rubbed it. I looked over to the nurse who was obviously relieved to have someone come to her side.

I said, "What is it, Maid Marion?" as I called her fre-quently. She frowned a big frown. I kissed her cheek and decided the best thing to do was talk to the nurse and see what had transpired.

On my way out of the small living room area, I turned to Marion and stuck my index finger in the air and bent it several times as if to say, "I will be right back, don't worry, I love you." Marion must have thought this was wonderful and mimicked my action immediately.

I spoke with the nurse and after we documented what had happened, I went to check on Marion again. She was mimicking the action I had just performed to the other residents in the room—holding her index finger in the air, bending it up and down, in a little wave.

"What is she doing?" asked the nurse.

"I think she is telling the others that she loves them," I said smiling.

The very next morning I discovered Marion waiting for me at the door. She smiled and hugged me and then made her finger sign for love. I smiled at her as the tears welled in my eyes. I could tell Marion had finally found a way to communicate what she had been longing to tell me: "I love you and thank you."

Eventually this sign of love spread throughout the unit like wildfire. All the residents and staff used the sign of love with Marion and with each other.

Marion proved love can be conveyed without words, and that Alzheimer's disease doesn't change a person's ability to share it.

Annisha Asaph

Katie

The wheelchair dwarfed her tiny body as she sat quietly hugging the teddy bear in her lap. Even though her hair was pulled back, soft wisps of rogue curls framed her face. All dressed in pink, Katie was the picture of sweetness.

It was obvious that Katie was a favorite among the nurses as gentle love pats were given each time they passed her chair. But even with the touches of love, she simply sat with her eyes focused on the floor. Well into her nineties, Katie was afflicted with Alzheimer's.

Sadly, Katie wasn't the only one in the room who was lost in her own world. There were fifteen others in varying degrees of dementia who had joined her in the activities room of the nursing home. And, for the next hour, this little group would be my "audience."

As a part of my Touch of Love ministry, I have the privilege of taking my little "sidekick" (dummy), Ezra, for visits in nursing homes, hospitals, and places of special needs. He sits on my lap and with the trickery of ventriloquism, he can say the darnedest things.

The scene was all too familiar . . . wheelchairs, walkers, blank faces, and weary bodies. But what was also familiar was the evidence of loving care given by the nurses and staff. I'd come to the conclusion that "TLC" is a universal, inborn quality in caregivers to the elderly.

As Ezra and I moved from wheelchair to wheelchair, the mood in the room changed. Not only were there sounds of laughter coming from the patients, but they were coming from the nurses as well as they witnessed the delight in the responses to Ezra. It seemed that everyone in the room was connecting with the fun—except for Katie.

She simply sat. Her eyes focused on the floor.

Having started on the opposite side of the room, we reached Katie's wheelchair. Kneeling in front of her, with Ezra at her eye level, Ezra said, "Hello, Katie. I love you!"

She lifted her sky blue eyes and said, "I love you too!"

It was breathtaking to watch the transformation in Katie's face as she broke into the most delightful toothless smile. And the "conversation" between Ezra and Katie? It was actually quite comical. The topics changed with every other sentence, and Ezra was having a hard time keeping up! It was obvious that in her younger days, Katie had a wonderful sense of humor, on full display here.

At first, because I was so focused on Ezra and Katie, I was unaware of the commotion happening behind her. But, gradually, I realized that something was going on. The nurses and staff were hugging one another . . . actually jumping up and down. They were laughing and crying at the same time, beckoning to others in the hallway. I wondered, *What good news have they just received?*

It wasn't until I had finished the visit that I learned the "good news" . . . it was Katie. That was the first time that any of them had heard her speak.

"Ezra may be a dummy, but he has accomplished something we haven't been able to in three years!"

Gail Wenos

Winter's Story

A mother's love for her child is like nothing else in the world.

Agatha Christie

December arrived and with it, the usual preparations for the holiday season. Our unit, an NICU, entered our hospital's holiday decorating contest. Snowflakes and all, my helper elves and I transformed our workplace, abiding by the theme "Peace on Earth and Goodwill to All."

Here in Scottsdale, Arizona, the daytime temperatures had dropped into the fifties. We had three solid days of rain, our equivalent of a midwestern snowstorm. The locals agreed that the last and coldest season of the year was upon us. Yet little did we know that winter was yet to arrive in our unit.

On December 5 during a scheduled Cesarean section for breech presentation, one of our neonatologists was urgently called to the operating room. All present were astonished by the baby who had just been born. Although crying and screaming, this little baby girl was encased in a thick layer of her own skin . . . her eyes merely narrow slits, her arms and legs flexed and contracted. It was as if this precious little girl had been born in a cocoon.

Our neonatologist immediately recognized this child as a *collodion* baby. She had seen this condition before and assured us that the yellow tight film, or dried collodion membrane, would undergo *desquamation* or peeling complete by two to three weeks of life. She assured the parents that although their baby would require special care, chances were that she would be okay.

Instinctively, the mother also knew that all would be fine as she received her child with open arms. Even through narrow slits, their eyes met and so did their hearts. Lovingly she named her new baby Winter.

I met Winter for the first time when she was three days old. When I approached her Isolette, I was shocked. I had never seen a baby like her in my nearly thirty years of experience. After report I had to step away and take time to compose myself. Several deep breaths later, I began my nurse-patient relationship with Winter, an experience I will never forget.

Cracking, leathery skin covered her entire body. She was able to move her arms and legs, yet range of motion was limited by the all-pervasive thick skin that restricted even the digits of her hands and feet. The same thick skin covered her ears, yet the ear canals were open. Winter's eyes were narrow slits and her face was encased in the thick skin, yet her nares were open and she required no supplemental oxygen. Remarkably, she was able to suck, swallow, and breathe easily.

Needless to say, her condition required special considerations. Initially she was kept in an Isolette with 90 percent humidity, more like Florida than Arizona. Nothing could be attached to her skin, no skin temperature probe or monitor electrodes. No arterial or venous access could be maintained, accept via a single umbilical catheter. Winter's care included protective isolation, sterile linen, rigorous skin care and diaper care, frequent application of emollients, lubricating eyedrops, and daily baths with gentle debridement.

Winter's mother breast-fed her around the clock. She participated fully in her care, eagerly making suggestions. After she was discharged, she came to the hospital in the morning and stayed all day despite her C-section and her two children at home. She pumped her milk diligently so that Winter rarely had formula, even during the night. Winter's dad spent long hours at work but visited in the evening and always told Winter how much he loved her. Grandparents provided support, visiting often and taking care of Winter's siblings.

After that first day, I became attached to Winter. I took care of her every day that I possibly could. Special babies with special families usually attract an entourage of nurses who insist on taking care of them. Winter had her posse. No outsiders had a chance.

Gradually, Winter started to emerge from her cocoon. She was acclimating to our dry desert environment and moved to a regular crib. Those beautiful dark eyes became larger. A great deal of her leathery skin shed. She had freer movement of her arms and legs. As the thick skin came away, fingers and toes also appeared. She could grasp. Her skin became accustomed to cotton clothing, cute, mostly pink little baby girl clothing. Soon her medical needs would be provided on an outpatient basis. Soon we would say good-bye.

As far as needs, Winter actually was born with everything she would ever need. Sure, her unusual condition required NICU care but she had all the things that any baby needs, all that any of us really needs—a mother who loves her and believes in her and knows that everything will be all right.

Christmas Eve arrived. It was time to go home. Winter was all dressed up in her layette and bonnet, sitting in her car seat and ready to go. Her mother gave me a long hug and thanked me for taking care of Winter, for doing so much for them. Tearfully, I hugged her back, looked into her eyes and told her that they had done so much for me. They had become *my* inspiration.

Each December we are reminded to think of "the real meaning" and "the true spirit." When snowflakes appear I will always remember a mother and her remarkable little girl. I will fondly recall Winter's story, one of love and belief, a story of Madonna and child.

Christine Linton

Serendipity?

Destiny is no matter of chance. It is a matter of choice. It is not a thing to be waited for, it is a thing to be achieved.

William Jennings Bryan

He shouldn't have been on my unit, but Medical was full and Orthopedics had a bed opening. I shouldn't have been his nurse, but the R.N. assigned to that wing called in sick for the evening, so the rest of us divided up her patient load. If he had been sick just two weeks later, I would have been gone, since I had already accepted a job at a different hospital in another city.

Our first meeting was a bit unusual; it involved two rather uncommon items: an aspirin suppository and a large hypodermic needle. Not what one would call standard "get to know you" equipment.

During my administration of his nasal douche, I remember saying something like, "I know this is uncomfortable, Mr. Nichols, but it has to be done." Where'd I get that little tidbit of bedside manner? Not very comforting when someone's squirting saline up your nose, I'm sure. Most of the time, he hid under the covers in 541-2 and clearly wanted to be left alone.

On any other shift, he would have been the most critical patient on my team, requiring the most attention. But the moon was full and any nurse knows what that can mean. The night was crazy! I had a biker, involved in a motorcycle accident, who had definite attitude issues. He was not adjusting well to the pins in his legs and entering his room meant ducking airborne bedpans. An elderly gentleman, recovering from hip replacement, was a tad disoriented. He hid chewing tobacco and spit it on the walls, the linens, the dresser, the bedside commode . . . and the nurses' white uniforms. Three units of blood were infusing down Hall #1, which necessitated countless vital signs and checks on the blood warmers. There were complicated dressing changes and one unexpected Code Blue. So, with these situations and the extraheavy patient census, it was impossible to do more than meet basic needs. It was a night of "no frills" patient care—no back rub, no bedtime snack, no teaching, no interaction for psychological assessment, nothing but ordered procedures and meds. High stress is definitely not the best environment under which to recognize and appreciate your future mate.

My shift ended at 11:00 PM and with patient needs now in the domain of the crew on night duty, my charting began. By 1:00 AM, heading home seemed remotely possible, when a nurse's aide stood at the desk with bundles of clean linens in her arms and reported that the patient in 541-2 had soaked the bed. I was shocked!

"That young man wet the bed? What happened?"

"Your aspirin suppository is what happened!" she laughed. "His fever finally broke."

Now the guilt started to set in, gnawing at my

conscience for being a basic nurse instead of a good nurse. Since he was awake anyway, and no doubt feeling better now that his temp was normal, I decided to go in and apologize for his less-than-five-star treatment.

Our eyes locked. There was instant electricity, a sense of "something's happening here." In that first relaxed moment of a totally insane night my internal voice murmured, "*He's* been my patient?" He later admitted to a similar voice that said, "*She's* been my nurse?"

Running a hand through his tousled mop of hair, he sighed, "Forgive me, this is the worst I've looked in my life." But somehow I just didn't notice.

In a whispered conversation, so as not to wake others, we got acquainted. As it turned out, all of our lives we had been crisscrossing and missing each other. He lived four houses down from my little cousin for whom I babysat. Time and again I had pushed her stroller past his yard and glanced at the boy playing in the Lone Ranger tent. As teens, he went to West High, I went to East, and we'd been at countless rival school functions simultaneously. I often joined friends after school at the local burger joint where, coincidentally, he was working the back grill. I shopped frequently at the corner store where he was a stock boy, and so it went, on and on.

"Can I call you when I go home?" he asked.

The professional voice in my head said, "No," but "Yes" came out of my mouth.

A few days later, after relating to my aunt the events of that evening, she asked, "How will you know if he's *the one*?"

Terrified of a commitment like marriage, I answered, "He'll bring me flowers on the first date." This was a safe declaration, because flowers were a social grace of the past, all but abandoned in the 1970s.

So, guess what he had in his hands when he showed up

at the door? Serendipity? I think not! Somewhere around coincidence number 101, a reasonable person must abandon the "accidental" theory in favor of true destiny, kismet.

His version of how we met is a bit more condensed. His story is that I saw his butt and it was love at first sight. Of course, as is sometimes the case with those of his gender, he tends to oversimplify things.

Over the passing of the last twenty-eight years, we've still enjoyed late-night, whispered conversations, but they've been a bit more intimate. And I can say that my love has deepened as the tables have turned, for he has nursed me through spinal surgeries and cancer, among other medical trials.

And when I have been ill and have felt it was the worst I've looked in my life, somehow he hasn't noticed.

Tori Nichols

Billie

The course of true love never did run smooth.

William Shakespeare

"It's time again, Andy, roll over please," said Billie, a registered nurse in the navy during WWII.

"At least it's you again. You are the best nurse at giving shots. Even the other guys say so," said Andy.

"I think I may be beating this malaria and dengue fever. I even walked for an hour this morning."

"Good for you, Andy. It will be important to get your strength and stamina back once the infection is gone."

"I can't wait to go dancing again, and Billie, I'd like to go dancing with you."

"I'd like that too," she said coyly. "And it's a good goal for you."

Andy began asking Billie about herself and her family whenever she came close to his bed or gave his frequent injections. He learned that Billie had been orphaned at age ten and had a younger brother and sister, but few other relatives. She loved school, did well in her studies, and tutored many children who lived in the houses in which she earned her room and board by cleaning and doing laundry. When she graduated from high school she had planned to become a teacher, until a friend invited her to check out the Mount Carmel Hospital Nursing Program. Billie decided to apply because "You lived at the hospital and meals were free." After completing her studies, she joined the U.S. Navy as a nurse.

Once Andy was well enough, he and Billie courted on the dance floor as often as possible. Their love grew even as the war and their roles in it became uncertain. Andy enjoyed the way Billie made all the soldiers forget, for a time at least, their severe wounds, or lost limbs or eyesight. She took them out for picnics on the hospital grounds and got them to sing or tell stories. Sometimes she would have them do impromptu skits, even putting makeup on them.

When Andy was considered rehabilitated, the Marine Corps decided to send him to preflight school. Andy knew he didn't want to lose Billie from his life. They were at the Claremont Hotel dancing as the Russ Morgan band played *Together* when he asked Billie to marry him.

She replied, "Yes," in a low whisper.

He gave her a bracelet with his initials on it, made from a piece of metal from a Japanese kamikaze plane, retrieved when he was on an island in the Pacific.

Andy left for flight school and Billie was ordered to the naval hospital at Pearl Harbor in late 1944. By this time she had been promoted to lieutenant and she was proud of that accomplishment. She felt nursing meant more than providing medical services and again worked hard coming up with ways to take the soldiers' focus off their wounds. She adapted to Hawaii, and made coconut-shell bras and grass skirts for them to wear as they did skits or songs. Going to the local beaches for outings and picnics also helped them forget their pain.

Almost daily letters kept Billie and Andy's romance alive—until he was critically injured in a car accident. The doctors told his parents he would likely not survive. Of course, he couldn't write to Billie for months and she began to wonder if he had changed his mind about her.

Fortunately one of Andy's nieces found out about Billie once he could talk a bit. She sent Billie a letter explaining what had happened. It seemed like the romance was going to continue for sure. Then one day Billie received this letter from Andy:

> *My condition is quite bad and I know it will take me ages to get back to a somewhat normal mode of living. Of course, I do not know exactly how my condition is, or if it will hamper me in the future. Therefore, I do not want to subject you to a life caring for a "sickly man." I love you, darling, in fact so much that I would sacrifice anything for you, but I do not want you to be burdened because of me.*

Billie answered quickly that her love could not make a burden of her life with him whatever his physical condition.

With this hope, Andy recovered, and after the war ended and Billie's enlistment was up, she met him in Laramie, Wyoming, where he was studying to be a geologist. They married ten days later.

Billie started working at the university clinic as a charge nurse. Then she worked as a volunteer school nurse in her children's school or in a doctor's office as head nurse until she was sixty-five. Many patients who had regularly scheduled shots would ask if their appointment was on a day Billie was working. "You are the best nurse at giving shots," they said.

She joined the Retired Nurses Association and volunteered

annually at the local health fair. Billie kept her nursing license active until she was seventy-five. The last year she had her license, people were still claiming, "You are the best nurse at giving shots." During her daily walks, she carried her blood pressure cuff and stethoscope because she monitored many of her neighbors' blood pressures along the way.

Andy died at a young fifty-eight. Long after, Billie's engagement bracelet was still seldom off her wrist. It broke just three weeks before she died.

Her two big questions during her final days were, "How do assisted-living staff expect to pass inspection with the way they make the beds?" And, "Kerrie, what's taking your dad so long to come pick me up for the dance?"

Kerrie G. Weitzel

No Reply

Being deeply loved by someone gives you strength, while loving someone deeply gives you courage.

Lao-tzu

I took my father, a congestive heart failure patient, to our local hospital emergency room. Wild television shows about ERs pale in comparison to this particular night. Chaos reigned.

Every cubicle was filled, so we were sent to a bed in a corridor, where we waited eight hours. Given the over-crowded situations, we were virtually on top of other patients, separated only by thin fabric curtains. Across from Dad, an elderly man lay apparently comatose. His wife stood beside him, holding his hand, gently stroking his arm. Doctors, nurses, technicians were in and out, asking her the usual litany of questions.

Finally, an authoritative figure in a white coat entered the room and pulled the drapes around the bed. But we could still hear. "Mr. Jones, Mr. Jones. Can you tell me where you are?"

No reply.
"Can you tell me who the president is?"
Again, no reply.
"What day is this?"
No reply.
"What year is this?"
No reply.
"Do you know what happened to you?"
No reply.
"Are you feeling pain?"
No reply.
"Can you hear me?"
No reply.
"Can you see my hand in front of your face?"
No reply.
Finally I heard the nurse gently ask, "What is the name of the woman you love?"

Softly, quiveringly, came a response from the throat of the elderly man. "Anna Marie."

Marlene Caroselli

4

CHALLENGES

When you are inspired by some great purpose, some extraordinary project, all of your thoughts break their bonds, your mind transcends limitations, your consciousness expands in every direction, and you find yourself in a new, great and wonderful world. Dormant forces, faculties and talents become alive and you discover yourself to be a greater person than you ever dreamed yourself to be.

Indian Philosopher Patanjali

Mirachelle

People are like stained-glass windows. They sparkle and shine when the sun is out, but when the darkness sets in, their true beauty is revealed only if there is a light within.

Elisabeth Kübler-Ross

Joel and Holly held hands as they always did . . . some of the very best medicine. I gently inserted the fine needle and began his chemotherapy treatment. Their baby was due soon. Joel was quiet, but Holly shared their hopes for the future. Now that Joel was completing treatments, we hoped he'd be in remission and have quality time with the new baby. He was discharged that day, with plans to attend a Lamaze class that night.

A few months later, on a warm spring day, Joel and Holly's baby was on the way. We oncology nurses were invited to labor and delivery.

We grieved to see Joel in a wheelchair, now on a morphine drip. His frail voice barely spoke. He took Holly's hand and smiled like any expectant father. Warm tears filled my eyes. We oncology nurses stayed to care for Joel as the L&D nurses cared for Holly. How blessed we were to be able to bring brief joy to this couple.

As labor progressed, both Holly and Joel napped. The sound of the clicking from the infusion pump relieving Joel's pain comforted me too. When the delivery was near, we moved Joel onto a stretcher, with all the clumsy equipment needed for him, and aligned it next to the delivery table.

Holly pushed with the strength of the warrior she was, and when their baby girl arrived, she was placed on Joel's chest. We all cried as the new mom and dad smiled.

"She's our beautiful baby girl," Joel said hoarsely.

"Her name is Mirachelle. A combination of Michelle and miracle," Holly explained. "We hadn't planned this baby . . . she is our miracle."

Their baby spent many days on the hospital bed with her father, which gave her mother the strength to cope.

Too soon Joel's battle was over.

Though this story happened many years ago, the memory of this meaningful event has not faded with time. Today's healthcare changes of short staffs and short stays make it improbable that it could ever happen again.

I truly hope I am wrong.

Ruth Bredbenner

Mother and Nurse

Enjoy what you can; endure what you must.

Goethe

On a sunny mid-December day, my two children, Hunter and Caitlin, and I were broadsided at an intersection known for accidents, even fatalities. An elderly woman ran a stop sign, crashing into our car on the passenger side, where the children were seat-belted in. We spun twice in the road. The horn blared. The airbags deployed. Our lives changed in seconds.

Hunter, in the front seat, looked at me with panic in his eyes. Blood from cuts trickled down his face and arms. I moaned, "It's okay, sweetie," then looked in the backseat at Caitlin. My world crumbled. Blood poured from her chin and mouth; her beautiful strawberry blond head sagged motionless against the backseat.

I jumped from the car, screaming, "Caitlin, Caitlin!" No response. I ran to her side of the car and leaned over the crumpled door, through the broken glass. She was unconscious and not breathing. I begged God not to take her and to put my nursing knowledge and skills into action. Holding her neck, I started rescue breathing for what seemed like an eternity. Her blood filled my mouth with each breath. I kept praying and breathing, praying and breathing. I repositioned her jaw, and she started to cough and gag just as the EMS arrived on the scene.

"I tried . . . I breathed," I cried to them. "I tried . . . "

"You saved her life," they said, guiding me away from the car.

I watched them work, sitting there on the ground, crying, praying, pleading with God. It was as if I were watching a movie, but the scene was real. A bystander called my husband at work to tell him the news. I can only imagine how he felt hearing the words, "Come. Now."

We were all taken away in different ambulances to the same hospital. I kept begging them, "Just take Caitlin in a helicopter to a trauma center."

"We need to stabilize her first in a closer hospital," they repeated. Finally, later, she was airlifted, in very bad shape, with multiple severe, life-threatening injuries.

I was soon discharged, but not before an ED nurse gave me paperwork, a prescription for pain . . . and one of Caitlin's front teeth.

We started for the hospital to be with Caitlin, but I felt like I had to go by our house to get a picture for the surgeons, and I had to change my clothes, stained with our daughter's blood.

The floor was strewn with Christmas wrapping paper, bows, and tape. We left the house, and the ride seemed to take forever. My heart as a mother was broken, my poor baby was near death. My nurse's head and heart kept hearing, *apneic at the scene, unconscious, closed head injury.*

Every mother's worst nightmare was made even more traumatic since I was an OR nurse. *Would I be able to give consent for organ donation? Would my husband agree? Could I bear to bury her in her little cheerleading uniform?*

Thank God, we would never have to make those heart-wrenching decisions.

Caitlin remained in the pediatric ICU until January 3, giving us many scares throughout her stay there. She was transferred to the floor for another week, then to children's rehab for an intensive, three-week therapy regimen. On February 5, she was discharged home for her brother's thirteenth birthday . . . and Christmas.

I thank God that she's the feisty, stoic, strong-willed, walking, talking, thirteen-year-old strawberry blond teenager that she is today. I'm also thankful to Him for fortifying me to perform as a nurse that fateful day.

A mother never thinks that after giving life to her child once through childbirth, there may come a time that she has a chance to do it again.

Mary Pennington

The Other Side of the Bed

My friends are my estate.

Emily Dickinson

It was the scariest day of my life. I sat next to the bed listening to the "beeps" of my newborn son's heartbeat. The ultrasound tech kept very quiet, but I had seen enough echocardiograms as a thoracic ICU nurse to know. I looked away from the screen and gasped back a sigh and a cry. The results were confirmed when the pediatrician stepped in and said that our son, Carson, had been born with four heart defects. I felt all the strength in my own heart slip away.

As I called my husband with the results, I realized that my place as a critical care nurse was about to change: I was moving to the other side of the bed.

I was used to being the one in control, the nurse who fixed things, who could rally in an emergency, who could do something. I couldn't do anything now but wait for six months until Carson had gained enough weight, or deteriorated enough, for the surgery to be performed.

So we waited. As Carson's skin color slowly became blue, I controlled everything I could. We researched and handpicked the surgeon, anesthesiologist, perfusionist, and hospital. We were ready, or so I thought.

On a Friday when three of my best friends and their children were at my home, the phone call came. Carson's most recent results showed he was declining more rapidly than we thought and the surgery needed to be moved up, fast.

"Oh, one more thing," the nurse added. "We need O positive, CMV negative blood donated for him."

What? How did I miss this key element? My husband and I had planned that one of us would donate blood for him. But we were different blood types. I hung up the phone and my friends' faces mirrored mine. I shared the news and two friends smiled and declared, "We have O positive blood!"

Jan and Denise drove off to donate blood, while Melinda and I took care of four babies under the age of six months and their four older siblings. We changed dirty diapers, wiped runny noses, and at one point Melinda breast-fed Denise's baby while I bottle-fed Jan's youngest. We laughed at the sharing of care between moms, so another mother could provide blood for my son.

Denise and Jan returned in a couple of hours with the news: Denise was CMV negative and her blood would be ideal for Carson!

The day of surgery was emotionally exhausting. My husband and I handed Carson over to the anesthesiologist and tears welled in our eyes, while knots knitted in our guts. Knowing too much can be a blessing and a curse. As I watched the clock, I knew when they would stop his heart, put him on bypass, make the repairs, restart his heart, and close his chest. Several excruciating hours later, the surgeon came out and announced that Carson's surgery had gone perfectly!

As I stood on the other side of the bed in the ICU, the nurse in me wanted to check the ventilator, his dressings, IVs, and chest tubes. Then, as the nurse hung Denise's blood over Carson's bed and the red drops ran down the tubing into his body, I realized why my role had changed. I wasn't out of control, as I thought. I instead trusted another nurse to stand in my place, just as Denise's blood dripped in the place of mine. Many nurses served as my substitute on the other side of the bed so I could just be "Mom" on my side.

That's when I realized the core of nursing is being there for each other . . . as nurses, mothers, and friends.

Cyndi S. Schatzman

A Dose of Compassion

There never was any heart truly great and generous that was not also tender and compassionate.

Robert South

Any first-year elementary teacher knows that half the children she sends to the nurse aren't sick at all. But what's a teacher to do? If she sends him and he isn't sick, he misses a math test. But if she doesn't send him and he is sick, he may throw up all over the classroom. It is that thought that makes even veteran teachers tremble.

So she sends little Johnny to the clinic. He practically skips down the hall with the clinic pass clutched tightly in his little fist. After five or ten minutes he returns to the classroom. The paraphernalia he brings back tells the story: two saltine crackers for a tummy ache, a Dixie cup with ice for a sore throat, or a Band-Aid for anything that involves even the most microscopic speck of blood. He walks back into class proudly displaying the proof that he was indeed declared to be in need of medical attention by a trained professional. At our school, her name is Nurse Janice.

I had been teaching for nine years when I was diagnosed with multiple sclerosis, a chronic and unpredictable disease. The diagnosis brought with it worry, and surprisingly, relief. It meant that there was a name for my suffering. There was a reason for my debilitating fatigue and weakness. But it also meant that life changes would occur over which I had no control.

Learning about the disease and how to cope with it filled my time and my thoughts. The fatigue was unbearable. No matter how much I slept or rested, I was still tired. On the outside I looked the same; no one would have suspected a thing. But the truth was, my health was deteriorating. Daily injections slowed the progression of the disease, but I was fighting an invisible enemy. And I hated it. I began losing strength in my right leg, which caused me to limp when I was tired. And when I started losing my balance, stumbling and staggering, it was just one more indignity to add to the list. Still, I bravely and stoically continued to teach.

After a lot of thought, I decided to tell only two people at work about my diagnosis: the principal and the school nurse.

"I want you to know just in case," I explained to Nurse Janice. "I don't expect anything to ever happen at work. But if it does you'll know my medical history."

"Thank you, Karen," she said, looking into my eyes. "And how are you with all of this?"

"I'm fine," I said, still in denial. "I'm fine. But I don't want anybody to know, okay?"

"This is between you and me," she promised.

A few months later, her promise would be tested. As I was hurrying across the classroom one day, I stumbled. In an instant I was falling. My arm slammed into a desk as I fell to the floor, where I landed on my stomach. A co-worker rushed to my side. Tears started to well as I slowly got up.

When I entered the clinic, Nurse Janice looked up. "Karen, what's wrong?"

"I fell," I managed to say.

"Keep an eye on the kids in the clinic," she said to the nearby receptionist.

She led me to an empty office next to the clinic and shut the door behind her. I sat down holding my arm as she knelt in front of me, gently wiggling my pant leg up to reveal a badly skinned knee. "This might sting a little," she said, putting ointment on it.

She asked questions and reassured me. Her eyes were kind and comforting. I felt as if I was her only patient, and that she had all the time in the world. She carefully bandaged my knee and then looked at my upper arm, which was already turning purple over an area the size of a brick.

She put her hand on mine and asked, "How are you?"

"Well, my arm is starting to hurt and . . . " I started.

"No," she said softly. "How *are* you?"

I knew her question wasn't about a skinned knee or a bruised arm. The question was deeper. My life had been turned upside down with the diagnosis of MS and I hadn't cried a single tear. But now I cried . . . and cried. I wept for lost dreams and an uncertain future. I sobbed deeply, from the core of my being. She consoled me, and then I cried some more. When the tears slowed and then finally stopped, she brought me a cold, wet paper towel to put over my swollen eyes.

"Take as much time as you need," she soothed.

When I was ready to reenter the world again, I followed her back to the clinic to get a bag of ice for my arm. Kids were lined up to see the nurse; one with tear-streaked cheeks, another holding her stomach, and a few more sat waiting to tell their stories.

As I walked out of the clinic, I glanced back and had to smile. Nurse Janice was on her knees, with the face of a small child cupped gently in her hands. *This is what she does day after day,* I thought. *Students come and go. Sick or not, they get a dose of compassion, a dose of kindness, and a listening ear. They get a moment to be the only one in the room.*

Healing takes place in that little clinic with the cartoon posters. It takes place while sitting on a green vinyl bed, with a nurse looking into the eyes of a child and listening, really listening, to what is said, and to what isn't said. And the cup of ice or saltine crackers he takes back to class may not prove to his teacher that he was truly hurting. But it is proof to one small child . . . and me . . . that in that moment, we are more important than anyone else in the world.

Karen Fisher-Alaniz

Chimes of Joy

The most profound joy has more of gravity than of gaiety in it.

Michel E. Montaigne

Most people, whether hospital staff, patients, or visitors, are familiar with "Code blue, code blue!" Those words summon up frightening and fearful feelings as staff are alerted to a medical emergency involving life and death.

Now, "The Chimes of Joy" are becoming familiar to many as well. After the birth of a baby, chimes are played over the paging system to get everyone's attention, then soft sounds of a lullaby float down each corridor of the hospital, announcing a new life. Many people benefit from this moment of happiness, but for two families it became a significant event in their lives.

In a hospital room on the medical floor a family held vigil. A woman with cancer, who had fought a brave battle for many months, was now gravely ill. This frail patient was at peace with God and had no fear of dying. Her family surrounded her with their love and support. When the nurses gently made them aware that the time was drawing close to her final breath, they each prepared themselves for the loss.

Then they heard the dying woman whisper, "I hope a new life comes into this world as I leave."

Within seconds, chimes played and a lullaby floated through the air as their mother smiled up at them, closed her tired eyes, and died serenely. Amazed and speechless, the family cried tears of sorrow and joy.

Feeling a bond with this newborn, the grieving relatives wanted to learn more about this perfectly timed birth. A few days later in the local newspaper, next to their mother's obituary, they spotted a birth announcement of the same date. They called the parents and carefully introduced themselves to the puzzled couple, sharing their poignant story. The new parents were delighted to hear from them and eventually graciously accepted the $100 gift and, in honor of the family's wife and mother, bought a savings bond for their son.

Years later, both families still exchange Christmas cards. The donor family sends the child a birthday card each year and his parents send them an annual photograph of him.

I was witness to the unfolding of the divine plan: to see the joy of birth lessen the pain of death.

Judy Bailey

Tom's Mountain

Courage and perseverance have a magical talisman, before which difficulties disappear and obstacles vanish into air.

John Quincy Adams

With a name like O'Malley you know I'm Irish. They say those of us with Irish blood have a fighting spirit. Well, I channeled my fighting into the spirit of adventure: I have climbed on mountains all over the world. I had always thought that Mount Everest was the tallest, toughest mountain. I was wrong. My older brother climbed one that was much taller and far more difficult.

His name is Tom. He's a brilliant and talented person, with a ton of that fighting Irish spirit. He graduated from high school at the age of fifteen and due to his accelerated abilities and excellence in both the classroom and in sports, he received both academic and athletic scholarships to college.

Tom is ten years older than I. As a child, at night when I became frightened or unable to sleep, I would notice

Tom's bedroom light on. It was as though he never slept. I would go into his room and he'd let me sit on his lap while he continued to study. When I woke in the morning, back in my own bed, he was already off to school, or his furniture moving job, or training for some wrestling match. Then at night he'd be back studying hard again.

Tom completed law school, married, and had two sons, Tim and Tommy. While returning home from Tommy's college graduation, the whole family was in an auto accident. Tommy was severely injured, and my brother lost his wife of twenty-five years and his son Tim.

Critical and in a coma, Tom underwent emergency brain surgery. If he survived, the doctors predicted certain and dramatic brain damage.

The entire family took shifts, staying at Tom's side. During my turn I would sit beside my brother each night, talking to him as if he could hear and understand me. Tom would lie motionless as I rubbed his arms and sang to him his favorite Irish songs.

One day when my sister Molly was with Tom, she called the family up: "Come to the hospital! Tom is dying."

All of his major body systems had begun to fail and the doctor suggested our family gather for our last good-byes.

Tom's climb seemed to be over.

Minutes turned to hours. Some forty-eight hours went by and I stayed with him as the others left to get some rest. I said, "You know, Tom, sometimes when I've been real sick or injured, all I could do was stick out my tongue or move my eyes."

Tom stuck out his tongue.

I ran out to the nurse's station and yelled, "Tom just stuck out his tongue! He stuck out his tongue!"

I could tell by the look on the nurse's face that she didn't believe me.

Quickly I pulled her into his room and she awkwardly

asked, "Mr. O'Malley, please stick out your tongue."

He didn't.

Then I thought maybe I had been hoping too hard. With tears running down my face I bent down closer to his ear and whispered, "Please, Tom, stick out your tongue again." There was a long pause . . . then he did.

As time passed, the diligent nurses helped him learn to communicate in a laborious process using an alphabet chart. First he communicated by blinking his eyes, and then he progressed to nodding his head for yes and no. The very first night we tried this, Tom indicated he wanted to ask something. After an exasperating hour of frustration, we figured out his question: "Do the doctors know they are working on a lawyer?"

That is when I knew he was still in there, climbing a mountain higher than I ever dreamed of attempting.

With the nurses' unrelenting efforts and encouragement, Tom made slow progress, step by tiny step. He began to speak, to sit up. We were thrilled the day they placed him in a wheelchair.

He was transferred to Craig Rehabilitation Hospital where another team of remarkable, committed nurses worked him past his limitations with a tenacity and courage I'd never seen on any climb.

One day, while he sat in his wheelchair, paralyzed on his left side, Tom said to his nurse, "Someday I'm going to run the Boulder Bolder."

Without hesitation, she said, "I'll see you there."

I wondered what false hope she might be giving him. He'd run that 10K with Sharon every year. But how could he ever do it again?

Every day, with his nurses' help, he pushed, pulled, and did whatever it took to take another step up his mountain. That fighting Irish spirit that served him so well in school and in bringing him back from his coma was the same spirit and driving force that pushed him beyond his tragedy.

One year later at the famous Boulder Bolder race, Tom crossed the finish line—so did his nurse—in memory of his wife, Sharon, and their son, Tim.

Brian O'Malley

To Kunuri and Back

To do anything in this world worth doing, we must not stand back shivering and thinking of the cold and danger, but jump in, and scramble through as well as we can.

Sydney Smith

It was November 15, 1950, when Mary and I stepped out of the army ambulance that had brought us from Pyongyang to Sunchon, North Korea, to join the 8076 MASH unit. We were the first nurse replacements for two burned-out nurses who would be sent back to Japan. The commanding officer greeted us with, "Are we glad to see you! What took you so long?"

We voiced our concern about both sides of the road being lined with southbound refugees. "What is going on? Are those Communist Chinese up to something?"

"Don't worry about it," he responded, "General McArthur assures us we'll all be home for Christmas."

The chief nurse showed us to our quarters. A lightbulb hanging from the middle of the tent provided a dim light, the only light. Olive-colored long johns, underwear, socks, and fatigues hung on a clothesline strung the length of the tent. The tent sagged so much, we could stand upright only down the middle, alongside the laundry. My cot sat next to a blood-spattered wall. I spread out my mummy bag.

Casualties were light the next ten days at Sunchon. On the day before Thanksgiving, we moved north to Kunuri, twenty miles from the Manchurian border. All the nurses rode in the ambulances in the long convoy of trucks. They had even loaded the piano on a truck. Getting a new hospital set up was a new experience for Mary and me. The staff slept in an old, shot-up schoolhouse; my cot next to a blood-covered wall.

A short time later, a cowbell rang outside the tent. "Formatin' time. Formatin' time," the colonel yelled.

"What do we do now?" I asked.

"A formation is a party. He wants everyone to celebrate our new nurses," Captain Henry told me. She was the nurse I was replacing, an older nurse whose husband had been killed in World War II.

There was a record player and a piano in the officers' club tent. We each brought our mess gear cup and it was filled with the usual party drink, a mixture of grapefruit juice and medical alcohol. It burned all the way down. Everyone jitterbugged to some jivey music, combat boots flying on the canvas floor.

News of the party for the new nurses traveled to other outfits, and soon the tent was crowded and the party was getting rowdier. Men bragged to each other about their poker-playing winnings as they downed their grapefruit-juice cocktails. Two men vying for my attention got in a fistfight. The party was getting wilder. It was time to crawl into my mummy bag.

The day before Thanksgiving, it was bitter cold in our living quarters. The weather was freezing and the oil heater in the middle of the room was quite inefficient.

We nurses headed up, mess gear in hand, to stand in the long line for Thanksgiving dinner, expecting the usual canned pork or beef and gravy, canned vegetables, biscuits, and fruit cocktail. To our surprise cans of sliced turkey, cranberries, sweet potatoes, dried mashed potatoes, gravy, biscuits, and red Jell-O with raw apples were served. Outside a broken window behind the kitchen, a Korean woman with a baby on her back was loading up the empty beef and gravy cans into her apron. The scrapings would be dinner for her family.

After we washed our mess gear, another nurse and I headed for the pre-op tent to start our twelve-hour night shift at 1900. Since we were expecting a quiet night, only fifty army cots were set up. We couldn't hear much artillery. But by nine o'clock litters were pouring in. Wounded soldiers, freezing cold and in shock, quickly filled up the fifty cots. By midnight the ground outside was covered with casualties waiting while additional tents were quickly set up. An extra supply of blankets covered the hypothermic, shot-up soldiers on the icy ground. The little oil heaters in the OR tents weren't much help, even when they worked. We nurses wore heavy jackets over layers of warm clothes, but couldn't wear gloves on our cold hands.

Before the night was over, the fifty anticipated wounded turned out to be over six hundred. Every available doctor, nurse, and corpsman worked feverishly, crawling around on the frozen tent floor, cutting off six or seven layers of sleeves and pant legs in order to take blood pressures and get blood transfusions started. There was no such thing as a type and crossmatch. Icy cold blood in glass containers infused in everyone. Sometimes four transfusions at once were pumped into the shocky patients. As soon as they had a pulse and blood pressure, off they went to the operating room, where their litter was the operating room table.

"This transfusion won't run. I'm sure it's in the vein. Will you try?"

"No use. He's gone."

The electric lights went out from time to time and the doctors had to use flashlights to complete the operation.

Wounded Communist Chinese prisoners started showing up, and we knew that what had been a fear was now a reality: the Chinese had hit.

By 0500 we heard our tanks were moving back, leaving us unprotected. I was too naive—and too busy—to be scared.

At 0700 I went off duty as I heard the colonel yelling into the inadequate telephone, "This is Red Hot Six. This is Red Hot Six," but I was too exhausted to be alarmed. I broke the ice on some water in my mess cup and brushed my teeth, put on my pajamas, crawled into my freezing mummy bag, pulled the blankets over my head, and fell asleep. At 0900, a nurse shook me and yelled, "Get dressed, pack up, and go back on duty so the day nurses can get packed. We're moving out."

The stench of gangrene greeted me as I walked into an isolation room. Some American prisoners had been rescued from the North Korean camp. Their feet were badly frozen, black, and gangrenous. They undoubtedly would have to be amputated later. As each new bunch of casualties came in, I asked them where they had been hit. One group said, "We were ambushed between Kunuri and Sunchon," which meant we were nearly surrounded. We certainly couldn't escape the way we had arrived, but had to take a much longer route in order to get to Pyongyang.

Nurses usually rode in ambulances when we moved, but this time all the ambulances were needed to evacuate the patients to a small, nearby airstrip where C-47s flew all the patients out. So we nurses rode in the back of an army truck, our knees crowded against the generator, which took up the center space. I kept my eyes on the mountainous horizon, thinking any minute the Chinese in their off-white quilted cotton uniforms would come swarming like ants to devour us. Travel was very slow on the clogged, bumpy dirt roads. It seemed we were always being delayed. At one point, the colonel chose to take the right fork in the road. We heard later that troops and convoys who took the left fork were trapped at a Communist roadblock, nearly all of them killed or taken prisoner.

We stopped briefly at the 8063 MASH for dinner. They were relieved that we hadn't been captured. We continued on during the long cold night, all of us uncomfortably cramped in the truck, wondering if we'd make it out alive.

We finally arrived at the 171st Evacuation Hospital in Pyongyang at 0300. The next day we moved and set up our evacuation hospital in South Korea.

We arrived there at lunchtime and, while eating in their mess hall, overheard the conversation at the next table.

"Isn't it terrible! All the nurses in the 8076 MASH were taken prisoner!"

"Are you sure? I heard they were all killed."

Mary and I turned to face them. "We're nurses from the 8076 MASH and we're very much alive."

Jean Kirnak

Back to Life

Life does not cease to be funny when people die any more than it ceases to be serious when people laugh.

George Bernard Shaw

As a 911 nurse, I was a part of a well-coordinated team of professionals that systematically assessed and treated cardiac arrests and other life-threatening events. On one particular call, we were dispatched to a pub near a local university to find a man in his late fifties receiving CPR from the fire department.

One of my first duties as the team leader was to assess the quality and effectiveness of the CPR by checking for a pulse. The victim was being intubated by a respiratory therapist, a fireman was doing chest compressions, and the other respiratory therapist was putting electrical leads on his chest. I could not get to his neck to check for a carotid pulse, so I unzipped the man's pants to gain access to the femoral pulse in his groin area.

After several defibrillator shocks, the man's pulse

stabilized and he was made ready for transport to the nearest hospital. I picked up supplies, empty syringes, and other medications so I could accompany him, and became aware of my surroundings for the first time.

Two male college students sat in a booth immediately adjacent to our resuscitation area. As I was leaving, I heard one of them say to the other, "I think I'd come back to life again, too, if she put her hands in my pants!"

L. Sue Booth

Stumbling onto Something Real

Life's greatest happiness is to be convinced we are loved.

Victor Hugo

I had just returned to Milwaukee after nine years in Colorado. Discouraged and brokenhearted after a failed engagement, I took a nursing position at a local hospice and enrolled in graduate school. I think that is how I got so many college degrees—whenever my life wasn't working, I went back to school.

About the third month on the job, a young man named Michael was admitted to the unit. Only thirty-three years old, he was dying of a brain tumor. An engineer and accomplished skydiver, Michael owned a business designing skydiving equipment. I was assigned to be his primary nurse.

I walked down the hall and entered Michael's room to get a psychosocial history before planning his care. He was reclining in a leather Barcalounger watching TV, his half-eaten tray of lunch food pushed to the side. He was paralyzed on the right side from the tumor; his cane leaned against his chair along with the nurse's call button.

After introducing myself, Michael made it clear that he preferred to be called by his nickname, Shoobie. He explained that all of his skydiving friends have nicknames: Wishbone, Charlie Oatmeal, Freakbrother, Wildman, and others. Pulling out a picture calendar showing skydivers linked in a star free-fall pattern, Shoobie described how they went to jump meets across the country, often living out of the back of a van.

"See, that's a 'twelve-man,'" he explained. "It's great! I've done it all. And I'm not done yet. You see, when I die, I'm going to roller-skate straight down Pikes Peak." Then he erupted in peels of laughter.

There was a knock on the door and eighteen people walked into the room, several carrying six-packs of beer. With every person in the suite looking at *me*, Shoobie asked if they could have a party. Never one to worry about rules, I assured them it was fine and closed the door on my way out.

Shoobie—always the host, always in a good mood, joking with his friends—shared many evenings like that with the skydivers. I was impressed at how many nice people he knew and how much they thought of him.

One evening after his friends left, he asked, "Why do you look so sad tonight?"

I soon found myself telling him about my failed engagement, and my history of dating losers.

"You need to find someone, a nice guy; a hero in your life."

"Yeah, I guess I do need to find a nice guy, but heroes are hard to find."

"We are all heroes to each other. You have helped me so much; you need to find someone that helps you. Like I said, you need to find a nice guy. Someone like Charlie Oatmeal."

Laughing out loud, I responded, "Charlie Oatmeal! He's not my type. He's too quiet, too soft-spoken. Don't be silly!"

Talking softly, Shoobie said, "Maybe the type you want isn't the type you need. Look for what you need." With that, he got into bed.

I thought carefully about what Shoobie had said. Maybe Shoobie came into my life for a reason, just as I had entered his. Maybe Shoobie was right. Perhaps what I needed wasn't what I had been looking for.

As we entered the dog days of summer, it was clear that Shoobie was deteriorating. Not as many friends came anymore and Shoobie had limited energy when they did. He began to have more and more days where he slept most of the day, and eventually was barely conscious. There were times the nursing staff thought he would die in his sleep, only to find him sitting up and lucid a couple of hours later.

After one particularly difficult day, the elevator doors opened and I intercepted Charlie Oatmeal as he started down the hall.

"Charlie, Shoobie really isn't doing very well. You may not want to stay."

He paused for a minute, and then looked me in the eyes. "Will he know if I am here?"

"Well yes, perhaps. They say even people in a coma can hear. He'll probably know you're here."

"Well, that is good enough for me. He might need me." He turned and started down the hall to Shoobie's room.

Charlie spent the next six hours sitting at the bedside, talking with Shoobie. Holding his hand, he related one skydiving story after another. When free, I went down to sit on the other side of the bed and listen. Occasionally, Shoobie would smile as Charlie talked of jumping nude into the Running Bear Nudist Colony or being stranded in a cornfield, miles from the drop zone.

"You know the best jumpsuits ever made were sewn by Shoobie," Charlie said to me. Shoobie smiled.

"No, I didn't know that," I said softly, watching carefully. Shoobie was right. There was something very special about Charlie. A special kind of person that sits at the side of his dying friend telling stories and making sure he is not alone. I found myself staring at Charlie as he comforted his friend that night. I was struck with the feeling that maybe this was the hero I had been waiting for.

Shoobie died two days later. He was given a skydiver's burial; the body cremated and the ashes taken to 10,000 feet. Charlie participated in the burial jump and described how the contents from the urn slowly rose in a spiral as a stream of light came down through the clouds.

The next week, Charlie called me and asked me out.

We were married the following spring, and honeymooned in Colorado. I could have sworn I heard roller skates when we were at the summit of Pikes Peak.

Barbara Bartlein

Do That Voodoo That You Do So Well

His eyes said it all. They had to. With a ventilator tube protruding from his mouth, Max couldn't tell me how awful the pain was, but I knew just by looking into those beautiful blue eyes that it was unbearable.

Max, my husband, had just undergone an eight-hour operation to replace his almost useless liver with one from an anonymous donor who had died just hours before. This incredible gift would give Max the possibility to live longer than his forty years. He would be able to watch our two children grow into adulthood and we would fulfill our dream of growing old together.

At the time Max received his transplant, doctors felt it unwise to give much pain medication after the surgery, giving the new liver a better chance of functioning properly. I'm sure they told us about this when they explained about the surgery but with so many details this one either went unheard—or we just didn't want to hear it.

That is how I found myself sitting in the recovery room watching the man I loved wracked with pain that no one could do anything to relieve. I felt powerless. I felt frustrated. I felt like I would go crazy. I had visions of running down the halls, screaming at the top of my lungs, and going right out the hospital door. I had never felt so helpless in my life. But Max needed me. I knew I had to pull myself together and do something other than nervously stroke his hand.

Why was I thinking so irrationally? After all, I was no stranger to stress and pain. Then it occurred to me. I knew what to do. I knew how to deal with pain. As a childbirth educator for the last fourteen years, I taught women how to cope with the pain of childbirth—and what pain could be worse than that? I knew the drill—take a deep breath and concentrate on relaxing.

In a soothing, yet firm voice, I said, "Max, you're going to have to listen to me and do exactly what I say. I believe I can help you deal with the pain."

This was a risk. Max had little use for our Lamaze classes when we were expecting our first child. In fact, he embarrassed me by falling asleep during most of them. Then, when I trained as a childbirth educator and began teaching classes myself, he used to tease that I was teaching these women "voodoo."

If I hadn't been so panicked, I'd probably have chuckled. Max was a "captive audience" and I was going to do my "voodoo" on him.

I began by using a common relaxation exercise. I talked our way through his body telling him to relax first his forehead and then his eyes; his cheeks and then his jaw; his neck and then his shoulders. I told him how he could relax his chest muscles and not fight the ventilator and how he could relax his abdominal muscles to ease the pain there. We went all through his body, relaxing each tight muscle all the way down to his toes.

At first it helped but soon the pain became apparent on his face again. I also could tell by the look in his eyes that he was a bit annoyed with my ordering him around, but I knew I had to keep trying to find something to help.

I then decided to use another pain management

technique that works well for laboring women—visualization. I began talking softly about a trip Max and I had taken years before to Martha's Vineyard. "See the boat ride over to the island and how we fed the seagulls midair." Then I went on to describe our room in the quaint little bed and breakfast. I talked about our walks along the shore. "Remember how the salty breeze felt on our faces, and how the sand squished beneath our feet?"

My voice was as shaky as I was feeling. But soon I was so lost in the memory that I forgot how scared and helpless I felt. The best part was that I could see that Max was starting to relax too. His face reflected the calmness I could feel flowing through his body. The hand that had tightly gripped mine was now just resting in my palm.

I knew the secret to making this kind of pain management technique really work was to incorporate all the senses in the images. Max needed to smell the smells, hear the sounds, feel the air on his skin, and see the beautiful, blue sky all in his mind's eye. And he did.

When I could sense that it was harder for him to pay attention and that he was beginning to suffer the pain again, I'd just switch stories. That night we relived every trip we'd ever taken together. When I ran out of those, I began describing trips we had fantasized about.

During that long night, Max would drift off to sleep and I did too. But when the pain woke him, I started in on another travelogue. One nurse even asked if I was his travel agent.

By the next day, Max's pain had eased and they were able to remove the ventilator. His first words were a scratchy, "I can't believe you used that stuff on me!"

But the twinkle in his eye thanked me for that "voodoo" that I did so well.

Karen Rowinsky

A Nurse's Prayer

Lord, as I go to work today
I sense that You are near.
Here on my knees, I bow my head
In hopes that You might hear.

Oh Lord, I'm just a simple nurse
And humbly now I pray
That with Your help, I will make
A difference today.

Let me give them comfort, Lord
At times when things are rough
And give me courage to go on
When I have had enough.

Let me say just one kind word
That, in sadness, brings a smile
And give me time, that with the lonely
I can talk a while.

Let me touch one single life.
Let me ease one single pain.

Let me lend my shoulder to cry upon
When tears freely fall like rain.

Lord, guide my simple words today
When it's answers that they seek.
Give me strength to carry on
When my body's tired and weak.

Let me ease one broken heart.
Let me soothe one crying child.
Give me calm when chaos breaks
And everything turns wild.

Ease the shaking of my hands.
My spirit, please renew.
And when it seems there is no hope
Let me put my faith in You.

Let them see compassion, Lord
Each time I shed a tear.
And when, in death, I hold their hand
Let them feel Your presence near.

I ask this all of You, dear Lord
As on my knees, I pray.
But most of all, I ask of You
Help me make it through the day!

Ruth Kephart

5

BEYOND THE CALL OF DUTY

There are risks and costs to a program of action. But they are far less than the long-range risk and costs of comfortable inaction.

John F. Kennedy

The Promise

For the promise is to you and your children and to all who are afar off, as many as the Lord our God will call.

Acts 2:39

It was my fifth year working on the telemetry unit. On this particular day, I was assigned to take care of Mr. E., an American Indian in his late forties. As I read the chart, I remembered him instantly because I had taken care of him before. I was the first nurse to admit him to our unit years ago. He was a father of four, ages six to nineteen. He lived on the Indian reservation with his close-knit family.

In the past years, he'd been diagnosed with diabetes and severe peripheral neuropathy. He was a very quiet, reserved man, but always had a grin and sparkle in his eyes when I asked about his children. He never complained or asked for anything, but eventually I knew his routine and was able to anticipate his needs.

As the years went by, he lost both legs and had to undergo dialysis treatments three times a week. Even if I was not his nurse and he was on our unit, I often dropped by his room to say hello.

This time, after I got the report from the night nurse, she said, "I don't know what else we can do; he's in a coma and the dopamine drip is the only thing that is keeping him alive."

I gave a deep sigh, thinking about his children.

As I entered his room, it was dark and a little bit chilly. Mr. E. was covered with a white sheet. I almost did not recognize him because he had lost a lot of weight. In the corner was his petite, teary-eyed wife, looking tired and helpless. I'd never met her before, so I introduced myself and told her that I knew her husband through the years of his hospitalizations.

Then I went to Mr. E. and leaned over and whispered my name into his ear.

There was no response.

Before I left the room, I asked his wife what I could get or do for her.

She said, "I know my husband is dying. I just want my sons to see him before he dies."

"Where are your sons?"

"In jail," she wept. She explained that the oldest one was in prison in Florence and the younger one was in juvenile jail in Phoenix. "The social worker said it's impossible for them to visit their father," she sobbed.

I gave her a hug, then bent down to whisper to Mr. E., "I promise that before my shift ends, I'm going to try as much as I can to have your sons come to see you. I know how much you love your kids."

I gave them both my reassurance and left the room.

I phoned the social worker. To get the son from Florence would cost more than $350 for transportation and a police escort. Plus it would take a day or two to process it.

Next I called the officer at the Maricopa County Jail. He

flatly declined my request for the younger son to see his father before he died.

I got the telephone number of the juvenile jail facility and asked to talk to the officer in charge.

"This is a matter of life and death. I need a big favor."

I asked the officer if he had children and he said he did. I stated that I was asking on behalf of Mr. E. to bring his son to the hospital before he died. I told him he was near death.

"I know his dad is just waiting to see his son for the last time. If security is an issue, I'll ask our security guards to assist you regarding inmate protocol. I'll be working until 7:30 PM. Please bring the boy. I beg you."

All through the shift I kept praying for a miracle. I watched the clock, waiting for security to call me.

Nothing.

The dopamine drip was almost empty and Mrs. E. refused to have another bag hung. "There's no use," she said.

It was 7:00 PM when I saw our two security officers come down the hall. One stood outside Mr. E.'s room. The other asked the family to step aside at least fifteen feet from the perimeter. After a few minutes, two uniformed police officers emerged escorting a handcuffed prisoner. Stifling my joy, I introduced myself. The officers listed the rules: the son would be handcuffed at all times with a police officer. No family was allowed to approach or touch him and had to stay at least fifteen feet away from him. I watched his mother and could feel her yearn to reach for him.

I agreed, then went to Mr. E. I whispered to him again, "It's almost the end of my shift and I was able to keep my promise to you. I have one of your sons."

I waved to the officer to let them enter the room. I talked to the mother waiting outside, so grateful she started to cry. The security officer stood stiffly at the door. Within minutes, the son and the police officer came out of the room.

I approached the son. "Is that all you can spare for your dying father, after all I did to let you come and see him for the last time? You go back in there and if you feel embarrassed to say anything out loud, whisper it to him and tell him how much you love him. He may not respond, but he can still hear. Ignore the officer . . . talk to your daddy."

The son went back into the room with the police officer. When they exited later, the boy was crying.

I approached the officer. "One last favor. Can his mother give him a hug?"

Without hesitation, he gave me a nod and waved for Mrs. E. to come. She threw her arms around her son and he clutched his mother like a lost little boy.

I stood with tears flowing down my cheeks. The staff, the security guards, and even the officers had tears in their eyes.

Mr. E. died an hour later.

Gina Hamor

I Can't Go to Heaven Yet

The manner of giving is worth more than the gift.

Pierre Corneille

"Wow, she has the most incredible blue eyes—they actually dance!" I said to her daughter the first time I saw Ms. Smith. She seemed to glow as she lay in front of a huge picture window in her daughter's home. She had the brightest smile and the baldest head—not a hair left from the prolonged chemotherapy. The medical profession had done all they could for this little lady from Kentucky. Her daughter had brought "Mom" to her home in Tennessee to care for her so she wouldn't die alone.

Her home was out in the boonies. It used to be a convenience store of some kind. It was a long and narrow house and every time I opened the door, I expected to hear a chime go off. When I arrived the first time, I knocked and a huge man came to the door. Her son-in-law looked like Charlie Daniels, without the cowboy hat, with tons of hair and whiskers. "Come right on in here," he ordered, but with a grin. With slightly more than a little apprehension, I followed him in and so did three cats and two dogs.

There was Ms. Smith in a hospital bed with her mouth full of miniature Reese's Peanut Butter Cups. My kind of woman! I introduced myself as her visiting nurse. She smiled a huge toothless smile. The chocolate ran down the wrinkles near the corners of her mouth.

"Would you like a Reese's Cup?" she asked.

"Are you kidding? If I won the lottery and they paid in either money or Reese's Cups, I'd be hard-pressed to make the choice!" I popped that peanut butter delicacy into my mouth.

She laughed. "I think we'll get along great!" She wasn't wrong.

Ms. Smith was short and round and could do very little for herself. Over the months I was there, she shared her life with me. She had seven children and only one grand-child. She had a son in prison who she knew she'd never see again. Her daughter was devoted to her. She'd crawl in the bed with her mom and rub her head to help ease the headaches from the growing tumor. Ever so slowly, Ms. Smith began to lose the faculties she had left.

One night she began to have difficulty breathing and her daughter called me in the wee hours of the morning. I jumped into my car and put on my emergency lights and got there in record time.

Her speech was slurred but she whispered, "I can't go to heaven yet."

I asked her if she was afraid.

"No, I can't go to heaven without my teeth."

What? I looked at her daughter and she explained that during the move from Kentucky they had lost her mother's dentures. I looked down at Ms. Smith, whose bright blue eyes were still dancing.

"I won't meet Jesus without my teeth," she firmly whispered.

I could have explained that we will be whole when we meet our Maker, but I could see that she wouldn't compromise on this. I bent down and softly said, "I promise I will get you some teeth."

I prayed all the way home. "Why did I promise her teeth, Lord? You've got to help me out here."

I caught a few hours' sleep, then pulled myself out of bed and headed to church with my family. During the sermon I looked ahead two pews and saw Sandra Hayes. The hair stood up on my arms. She was a dentist, in practice with her husband. After the service I approached her, told her my dilemma, and asked if she could help. She agreed on the spot. I explained that in all likelihood she would not be paid.

"This family has no extra money. They live in the American version of the Outback," I cautioned.

Not surprisingly, Dr. Hayes said, "I'd be honored to help."

The next day she followed me to Ms. Smith's home and stirred up her stuff to make the dental molds, refusing to take any shortcuts. When Ms. Smith entered the gates, she'd have the finest teeth of anyone who'd ever passed through.

The following day Ms. Smith went into a coma. It certainly didn't look like she'd live to get her teeth because the denture process took four to five days. We were all disheartened, but we kept a vigil at her bed. I could see the weariness and love in her children's eyes as they turned her or patted her. We all talked to her, unsure if she could hear. The first day passed and she remained with us. Then a second, and a third.

Her daughter turned to me that evening and said, "I think she's waiting on her teeth."

"Yes, I think she is," I sighed.

I had called Dr. Hayes daily with updates on Ms. Smith's condition. She explained that she sends her teeth to a town about thirty miles away for a baking process to make them hard. She was bugging the poor "baker" and even offered to drive there to pick them up.

Finally the dentures arrived and Dr. Hayes wanted the honor of giving them to Ms. Smith. Occasionally during her comalike state Ms. Smith had opened her eyes. Now they were dim and glassed over. But when Dr. Hayes placed those teeth in her mouth, those beautiful blue eyes danced once more.

As we prepared to leave I handed Dr. Hayes the forms to complete for payment. "No charge," she said softly, then nodded toward Ms. Smith laying with a peaceful smile on her face. "I've already been paid."

Five hours after receiving her precious gift from Dr. Hayes, Ms. Smith died quietly in her sleep. I can only imagine how proud she must have been as she smiled in awe at her Maker.

Sue Henley

"Yes, they're my own teeth. I paid the dentist for them."

Making the Grade

It is not so much our friends' help that helps us as the confidence of their help.

Epicurus

This was going to be a great group of students—I could tell. I asked each one to introduce herself and tell us why she wanted to learn to be a certified nurse assistant. A few said this would be their first experience in health care, and they weren't sure what to expect. However, most of the students said this class would be their first step on the way to nursing school.

Marie caught my attention. She was a tall woman. She said she joined the class because she had been a home health aide for so many years; she felt she owed it to herself to achieve certification and earn the salary she thought she deserved. Later in the semester she confided to me that she wanted certification for her own self-esteem—she was tired of her family's constant teasing and criticism. She told me that they repeatedly called her "dumb" and said she would never amount to anything.

For the first two weeks Marie shone. She participated in class discussions and described techniques that could only have come from experience and creativity; these methods of patient care were certainly not in any text-books. She sailed through the clinical labs. With no need to practice bed baths or patient positioning, Marie would share her experience with classmates who were learning these tasks for the first time. Everyone in the class warmed to her and appreciated her kind and friendly disposition. So I was shocked when I administered the first written test and she failed—badly.

I spoke to Marie privately. She claimed she was just nervous and would try harder. But she failed the next two tests.

I approached Tanya, our admissions counselor, for advice. "I wondered how long it would take you to ask. Marie can't read very well. That's why she's not passing the tests even though she knows the material. Plus, Marie has no self-confidence in her abilities and talks herself out of succeeding. It would really be wonderful if you could find a way to help her earn her certification. She really has so much to offer, and passing the certification exam might help her believe it."

Of course, certification was important to *all* the students, but Marie was a gentle, knowledgeable caregiver who really needed—and deserved—to pass. How could I get her through the state exam? Her clinical demonstration would be a breeze, but the written exam would stop her cold. Then I remembered something from my original school orientation and inquired, "Doesn't the state give an *oral* version of the exam in some cases?"

Tanya said they did.

"Then I'm going to ask Marie if she wants to try that testing format. I'll read the next exam to her and see what happens. If she's willing to pay the additional fee for the oral exam, that might make a difference."

What about the rest of my students? Certainly they would need to be monitored during the test. If I read aloud they might be distracted. I had no answer then, and by the time of their next exam I was still seeking a solution. So with Marie's permission I posed the question to my students. Their response was immediate and unanimous. They glanced at each other, then stood up and changed their seats so no one would be sitting next to another student. One student beamed at me and said, "Go ahead, Mrs. Malkin. Just sit out in the hall with Marie. You can watch us from there and see that we aren't talking to each other. We really *want* to know if we understand this material. You can trust us."

And I did. I peeked into the classroom between the questions I read to Marie. Tanya also passed the classroom from time to time to see what we had worked out. All of the students were as good as their word. Marie scored over 80 percent on that first oral test, and on the rest of the tests that semester. She developed a comfort level with that testing style and continued to excel in her clinical work. By the time the students went to a local nursing home for their bedside experience, everyone wanted to pair off with Marie. We all delighted in her newfound confidence.

The day of the state exam I was as nervous as the students. Although I was not scheduled to work, I came in anyway "to straighten up," fussing around my classroom, rearranging shelves, and refolding linen while I waited for the students to finish. One by one they filtered into the room with certificates, hugs, and smiles. I congratulated all of them. Although they could have left upon completion of their exams, everyone remained on the pretense of helping me until we'd heard the entire class's results.

They were so relieved the exam was over they started talking nonstop. There was so much noise and chatter that we didn't notice when Marie appeared, standing quietly in the doorway. There was no expression on her face and my heart dropped. As the students began noticing her, the room slowly became silent. When Marie knew she had our complete attention she broke into a huge grin, strode into the room flourishing her certificate, and swept me up in an enormous bear hug.

Everyone cheered, and I could hardly breathe! She put me down and held her certificate in the air. "Look at this! Look at me! I'm going to carry this with me for the rest of my life, and if anyone ever tells me I'm nothing, why, I'll just pull this out and show them that I am really something!"

Susan Fae Malkin

The New Grad

Each person has an ideal, a hope, a dream which represents the soul. We must give to it the warmth of love, the light of understanding and the essence of encouragement.

Colby Dorr Dam

Startled by commotion, the young registered nurse, Janeen, entered the intensive care unit of Long Beach Memorial Hospital to begin her morning shift.

"What's going on?" she exclaimed as she watched a doctor, nurse, and respiratory therapist working feverishly over a new patient.

Having only completed nursing school four months earlier and still considered a "new grad," never before had she truly experienced such traumatic care in action.

The patient was a young female with an endotracheal tube connected to a ventilator, filled with fluid. Must be pulmonary edema, Janeen surmised. Wearing a neck collar, and in traction, the female's legs were elevated. Her discolored feet stuck out from under the sheets, a sign of poor blood circulation.

The new grad's attention was drawn to a middle-aged woman standing near the activity, appearing alone and helpless. With an overwhelmed and distraught countenance, the woman's bright green eyes blurred with tears while she watched her daughter's heart monitor. At once, a deep wave of sympathy swept over Janeen.

"What's going on?" the young R.N. repeated. She learned the young woman had been run over by a Ford Ranger truck while bicycling. She had fractured 111 long bones; many short, flat, and irregular-shaped ones; her pelvis; and her cervical spine, which could result in paralysis. Tire tracks were still visible on her chest. Her heart's papillary muscle was destroyed and her mitral valve was ripped almost entirely off. Her liver was severely lacerated.

When Janeen heard that the patient's twenty-third birthday had just passed two weeks before, she thought, *She's only one month older than me.* But, before her thoughts continued, she was interrupted by the yell, "Cardiac arrest!"

Orders were shouted. "Quick! Prep her for surgery."

The heart surgeon approached the mother. "Sibylle," he began, "we don't think she'll survive, but we're sure she'll die if we don't try."

Her tearful mother signed the consent.

As they transferred the young lady to the operating room, a priest gave her last rites.

Knowing that saving her would require a miracle, silently Janeen prayed, *If You do miracles God, please let one be visible today.*

After ten hours of surgery, doctors said it was a miracle. Now with a pig valve, the patient's chest was too swollen to close so a transparent thin film covered it.

For the next few days, Janeen continued to pray.

One morning, her eyes widened as she read the female's name among her list of assigned patients. She entered the room and introduced herself. "I'll be your primary care nurse. I'll take good care of you," then, turning to the mother who had traveled far to sleep at her daughter's bedside, she added, "and you."

Unprepared for the shock of seeing the patient's toes turn completely black, Janeen composed herself and continued to follow the orthopedic surgeon's instructions to take her to hyperbaric twice daily for oxygen therapy. Hopefully they could stop the gangrene from traveling and prevent amputation.

Janeen felt sadness on the day the patient heard, "We have to amputate all ten toes." But after surgery, she knew it was another miracle that the woman's legs were saved.

Saving the rest of her entailed a total of seventeen more surgeries. Many times, she had come close to dying. Once, a yeast infection developed in her blood, nearly killing her. Twice her ventilator alarm sounded, signaling that she wasn't receiving oxygen.

All of this brought unexpected emotions to the new grad. She worried the young lady would be forever dependent on the ventilator. All attempts to wean her off it had failed.

But again Janeen's prayer was answered. One day a doctor was changing her tracheal tube and was unable to insert the new one. He exclaimed, "I can't believe it, your incision has closed, and you're breathing fine!"

Another celebration day arrived three months later when the patient was transferred from ICU to a recuperative unit.

Janeen promised the patient and her mother, "I'll come to visit." And she continued visiting when the patient began rehabilitation two weeks later.

After completing two more months of rehab, with her

left leg one inch shorter than the right, the young woman finally hobbled out of Memorial Hospital. Now being called a "walking miracle," she and Janeen kept in contact.

A few months later, Janeen was thrilled to have her former patient as a guest at her wedding.

Nine years passed, and again she was thrilled as she watched the "walking miracle" march down the aisle to also be wed.

At the reception, Janeen enjoyed visiting with Sibylle, this time for a joyous reason.

And to this day, as a writer and speaker, I'm still grateful that Janeen is my cherished friend! Through my nine more operations, Janeen has continued to be my prayer warrior and encourager.

Vanessa Bruce Ingold

John Doe

I came to realize that life lived to help others is the only one that matters and that it is my duty. . . . This is my highest and best use as a human.

Ben Stein

I was a home health nurse coming home after an assignment when I came upon a small white car that had flipped onto its top and was resting in the middle of a deserted, poorly lit county road. I jumped from my car just as a middle-aged man crawled out.

"Are you okay?" I asked.

"I think I'm okay. Just shook up, but I think I hit someone on a bicycle back there! I swerved to miss him and that's when the car rolled."

The shaken driver pointed down the darkened road in the direction from where I had just traveled. I asked a passerby to call 911 and started down the roadside ditch in search of the bicycler. Approximately 200 feet later, I came across the body of a large, muscular, blond male, who looked to be in his midthirties, clad only in his tennis shoes and shorts, lying facedown in the grass and weeds.

I checked for a pulse, but could not find one. I yelled for help to log-roll him onto his back so I could recheck for a pulse. Another passerby helped me turn him, being careful to keep his spine aligned. The injured man was bleeding from his mouth and ears. When I still couldn't locate a pulse, I initiated CPR, and was rewarded with a return of a pulse by the time the rescue crew arrived. The man was taken immediately to University Medical Center, the only trauma-one center located in downtown Jacksonville, Florida.

Several days later, I noted in the local paper that a young man fitting the description of the one I had resuscitated had died after being struck by a car while on his bicycle. When I went to visit my parents and brother in Brunswick, Georgia, I recounted my story of trying to save his life. This was at the height of AIDS awareness when its dire consequences were felt to be a certain death sentence. I have a nervous habit of biting the inside of my mouth, so I said to them, "I don't know anything about the young man, except for his name. I should probably be tested for AIDS in six months or so."

I tried not to worry as I went on with my life, but the nagging threat remained.

Several weeks later I received a phone call from a woman who identified herself as the wife of the man I had attempted to resuscitate.

"How did you find me?" I asked, dumbfounded. No one at the scene had taken my name or my phone number.

The woman explained that she had a first cousin who was an electrician at the navy base in another state where my brother, also an electrician, had been discussing the accident. My brother mentioned his sister had resuscitated a "John Doe" who'd been struck by a car while riding his bicycle, and the cousin realized that it was his relative who was the victim.

"Thank you so much for trying so hard to save him," the woman said through obvious tears. "I'm a 911 dispatcher, so I know a little about how that must have been for you." She paused. "He was a wonderful man; I want you to know about him."

She went on to share how they'd been best friends since they were twelve years old. "He gave me a cigar wrapper as a ring to show his devotion," she chuckled. "We were married for seventeen years. He was a baseball coach for our three boys and a volunteer fireman. Sometimes he had trouble sleeping at night and would take a bicycle ride to unwind; that's what happened on the night of his accident."

I heard her catch her breath before she recounted how he'd never regained consciousness and was brain-dead. The family decided to removed life support and fulfill his wishes to become an organ donor.

"Thanks for resuscitating him . . . you helped make his wish come true."

Then, as if she'd been reading my mind, she added, "We loved only each other, exclusively, our whole lives. You needn't worry about anything affecting your health."

A wave of relief washed over me.

Only nurses could believe that all these mysterious coincidences could not be coincidences at all.

L. Sue Booth

A Heart for Haiti

It is one of the beautiful compensations of this life that no one can sincerely try to help another without helping himself.

Charles Dudley

My dream became reality when the Boeing 737 landed in Port-au-Prince, Haiti. Fifteen years earlier, as a teenager, I'd come to this impoverished island on a mission trip. Ever since, I'd longed to return as a nurse to help these people with no access to quality health care.

I packed as many questions as clothes for this trip. *Will we be safe? Where will we stay? As a pediatric and neonatal intensive care nurse, will I be able to assist in surgery? How will my family manage without me for a week? Can I really make a difference?*

I quickly learned our hosts would keep us very safe. The Haitian pastor and his wife, who run Mountain Top Ministries, go the extra mile to put their guests at ease—even a spoiled American like me. We slept on comfortable beds and ate tasty, healthy Haitian food.

The village of Gramothe, about eleven miles southeast of Port-au-Prince, had suffered extreme poverty for years. When Mountain Top Ministries began, the villagers, sustained by meager farming, had no school, no church, and no employment prospects. These talented, smart, family-minded people were trapped in a life with no opportunities—or hope. By the time our medical team arrived, the Haitian pastor had started a school, a church, and a small clinic. Employment and hope were on the rise.

We worked in a cinder-block building with open windows and no electricity, treating children with scabies, worms, and other parasites. Adults came with high blood pressure, diabetes, and numerous medical and surgical needs. We brought with us medications unavailable in this part of Haiti.

Our team of eighteen included three doctors, four nurses, and eleven nonmedical personnel to serve where needed. My good friend Karen, who had recently retired, came with a desire to help the forgotten poor. Both of us felt a little nervous. She had no medical training, and I wondered if I could step into the surgical assisting role. Soon we both felt comfortable with the diverse challenges.

The third day of patient care, Sonia, a beautiful nineteen-year-old, presented with a huge infected cyst on her neck. The mass, about the size of a baseball, protruded above her clavicle and extended to her larynx. Through our interpreter, we learned the lesion had appeared several years earlier. A Haitian doctor removed it, but it returned after a few months. Sonia then sought the care of the voodoo witch doctor who treated it with traditional methods. It worsened. Ostracized by her village, Sonia struggled to survive.

I assessed her condition. Pus dripped from the infected cyst, producing a putrid odor. With no access to bandages, Sonia had covered it with a leaf to absorb the chronic drainage. But she couldn't cover—or escape from—the smell.

When the surgeon examined Sonia, he knew he must excise the cyst. Karen and I prepped and draped her neck. Dr. Kothari injected 1 percent lidocaine with epinephrine around the area. He held the scalpel, paused a moment, put on a mask with a full visor attached, and continued. As he made the horizontal incision, a stream of yellow fluid shot up, covering his entire visor.

A powerful stench filled the clinic—and sent Karen running! The surgeon replaced his visor and completed the half-hour surgery. After he finished the last stitches, Sonia sat up and smiled. Through an interpreter, we explained the post-op instructions. I handed her the package of dressings, antibiotics, and pain medications, and gave her a hug. Then my own emotions surprised me. Although glad to have given her something she could not have otherwise received, I felt sad that I'd never see her again.

One year later, my husband and I led another medical team to Haiti. During the week of clinic, we toured the village and noticed the church choir practicing, so we took a few minutes to relish a native Creole song. Drawn to a lovely voice, I observed a young lady in the front row. I saw a horizontal scar on her neck. There, right in front of me, stood Sonia!

As soon as the song was over, I rushed up to talk to her. She smiled proudly, displayed her scar, and told us about the changes in her life since we helped her. She'd responded well after surgery, and the cyst did not return. She married and became a mother. Sonia also experienced spiritual healing with faith in Jesus and her eyes sparkled when she told us how she and her husband actively participated in church work.

I smiled as a great peace and joy accompanied me back

to the clinic. As I contemplated our work there, I realized the results were far more than medical. Not only was Sonia's life enriched, so was mine.

Anna M. DeWitt
as told to Twink DeWitt

[EDITORS' NOTE: *To learn more about and support Mountain Top Ministries, see www.mountaintopministries-haiti.org.*]

MERCI

Never doubt that a small group of thoughtful, committed people can change the world. Indeed, it is the only thing that ever has.

Margaret Mead

She was five years old when she made the trip from Czechoslovakia to the United States of America with her mother, sister, and brother. Helen still remembers meeting her father, waiting for them at Ellis Island, as they came through on the Queen Mary. He fought against the Bolsheviks at the age of sixteen as a soldier in the Ukrainian army. Near the end of the Second World War he decided to immigrate to the United States, a country he called "the country of last hope." He loved the freedom in the United States, but he and Helen's mother spoke sadly of their native homeland where they left everything, family and friends, to escape a totalitarian regime. Helen grew up hearing so many horror stories about people in need because of war. That's likely why she became a nurse.

In early 1991, her operating room manager at the University of Virginia said, "Helen, I'd like you to take on a little project."

"Okay," Helen naively agreed. "What's up?"

"Our nineteen operating rooms here are generating too much waste . . . clean stuff they haven't used . . . and it's very expensive to incinerate. With your twenty years in the OR, you have the knowledge and experience to figure out what to do with it all. "

So for a year, Helen collected clean medical supplies from all their operating rooms and donated them to missions. She researched the issue of RMW (regulated medical waste) and spoke to every expert she could find on this issue. She was appalled to learn that more than 2.4 million tons of hospital waste is generated in the United States annually, with the operating rooms being the largest waste generators.

"This is gold waste," she said, coining her own new phrase.

Helen worked four ten-hour days in the operating room, then spent countless hours networking with people on behalf of missions. Before she could say, "How did I get myself into this?" she had formed MERCI: Medical Equipment Recovery of Clean Inventory.

MERCI began receiving wish lists from many small mission groups. Helen never promised anything to anyone, but she did promise to work as hard as she could to fill their requests.

For years she sorted supplies after work, every day and on weekends. In July 1995, she was given one day a week for her "little project." By 1997, MERCI had a steady stream of volunteers helping to sort, and the results have been beyond their wildest imaginations.

Since Helen started this "little project," MERCI has captured and diverted more than *350 tons* of clean medical supplies valued at $75 million, and sent them all over the world. Another 50-plus tons have been donated to the University of Virginia research labs and to surgeons' mission trips.

When a local private hospital switched to powder-free gloves, they donated several skids of powdered gloves for a physician to ship to his sister hospital in the Ukraine. "In the Ukraine," he said, "doctors are doing rectal exams without any gloves."

When MERCI shipped 6,000 pounds of supplies to a hospital in Lithuania, a nearby hospital came up with 80,000 more pounds for them! Helen networked with a mission who paid to ship all 86,000 pounds. Soon after, another contact donated $200,000 of medical supplies to a Russian endeavor, then paid to ship the supplies there.

When she heard a clinic in Haiti needed a sterilizer, Helen wrote for nine months to a supplier who finally donated one.

Christian Relief, Advancing the Nations, Helping Hands, Operation Smile, Crosslinks, and Equipping the Saints are only a few of the many missions that have received medical goods from MERCI.

A nurse who helped Helen sort supplies for ten years saw a need for a hospital in Bolivia. MERCI donated thousands of pounds to this effort. Eventually, with the help of donations, the nurse bought a hospital in Bolivia and had the grand opening in July 2002. The story got even better when a local pediatric surgeon and the hospital donated free services to perform an operation on a small Bolivian child who suffered with an imperforated anus.

Over the years, Helen has presented the work of MERCI at the National Institutes of Health, and to the National Association of Physicians for the Environment, where MERCI was cited as a best practice. She has sat on a task force on Medical Waste Minimization per the request of her congressman. She spoke at Health Care Without Harm conferences, the Environmental Protection Agency Region III Environmental Colloquium, and to the Department of Health and Human Services in Washington, D.C. She was asked to help with a humanitarian initiative and to submit a proposal on how a MERCI-like template can be used at the federal level.

Before she retires in a few years, she's on another mission—to get every hospital in the United States to adopt a MERCI program. Helen says, "Can you imagine the good they could do if every unit on every hospital joined in?

"I pray our nation never comes under attack, has an influenza crisis, or suffers a grave natural disaster. FEMA, the Red Cross, and other relief organizations would not be able to provide enough first-aid supplies to the masses. But if there were a MERCI-like program throughout the United States, it would be the conduit for clean medical supplies to every local church in every community."

Helen's MERCI program still has no budget and the office is still in her home. She still works in a small area off of a loading dock. But she's confident that when her sister- and brotherhood of nurses learn about MERCI, they'll have a warehouse, website, and worldwide relief!

Helen French
as told to LeAnn Thieman

[EDITORS' NOTE: *To learn about MERCI and how it can be implemented at your healthcare facility, visit www.merci-medical supplies.com.*]

A Relay of Control

Love is all we have, the only way that each can help the other.

Euripides

It was with sadness and dread that I received a phone call from one of our hospital discharge planners telling me a patient, Joyce, had gone home and wanted me to call her. Joyce was a former coworker with me in another agency and was, ironically, their first hospice nurse.

I knew Joyce had been living with breast cancer for the past five years and had undergone a bone marrow transplant and multiple courses of chemotherapy. I had renewed my relationship with her a few years earlier when she was chairperson for the American Cancer Society's Relay for Life. Our hospice team participated in this twenty-four-hour fund-raiser. Joyce's energy and enthusiasm were contagious.

I called this wonderfully vivacious and funny lady and agreed, with a heavy heart, to come to her home. She said she understood that I managed the hospice program and would be coming in that context.

The next day I visited her and spent about three hours with her and her mother. Her husband, Steve, came home on his lunch break and we talked at length about Joyce's disease and the services of hospice. Joyce was not ready to give up the fight. She was only forty-seven years old (my age), a wife, and the mother of three young children. She was still convinced she would beat this disease. About a week later, after several more calls from family and friends, Joyce agreed to hospice care. She asked if I would be her nurse and I reluctantly told her I could not, because as the manager, I wouldn't be able to give her my full attention. However, I would come and see her as her friend.

And so began my visits, at least once or twice a week. Each was a spiritual experience. Joyce and I practiced the same religion and had strong faith. We also loved angels and believed in their presence and guidance. Despite her faith, Joyce struggled with accepting her impending death, determined she would live to see her three children grown.

During one of my visits, I told her that the hospice team would march in the St. Patrick's Day Parade to advertise the Relay for Life. I told her the Hospice Clowns (of which I am one) would also be there. "I hope you and your family can come and watch," I coaxed.

With that mischievous twinkle in her eye, she said, "I'll be marching with you. After all my years of working on that race, I'm not about to just watch it."

During the ensuing month, though, Joyce started to decline. She became weaker and weaker and, at times, confused. She still insisted she was not going to die and was very frustrated when others tried to be more realistic. Finally, one day she cried out in anguish, "I can't die! I just can't!"

I held her bony hand in mine. "Joyce, please put yourself in God's hands and trust that He will lead you in whichever direction you should go. You can control what you can, and the rest you have to leave up to Him and His angels."

A remarkable sense of peace came over her and from that day on she seemed to accept her fate. She slept more and more each day until finally I received a call from her friend, Linda, asking me to come. Joyce was not responding and the family was unsure what to do.

"I'm in my car only about a mile from Joyce's house," I told Linda. "But I'm dressed as a clown because I was headed for the parade." I asked her to prepare the family for my appearance at this heart-wrenching time.

I arrived to find Joyce in a coma and knew by her symptoms that death was near. As the tears rolled down my face, I said, "Joyce, you're still in control; you couldn't get to the parade so you brought the parade to you." I made sure she was comfortable, then told the family, "I need to walk the parade—for Joyce." Privately I told Linda, "Page me if she dies before I get back."

Halfway through the parade my pager rang. Ironically, I was again about one mile from her home. I removed my wig, wiped at my makeup, and went back to Joyce's to give the pronouncement and console her family.

As I drove home and the tears continued to flow, I had an overwhelming sense that Joyce had joined God and His angels in controlling the events of the day. They sent in a clown.

Flo LeClair

The Tale of the Sale

Let no one ever come to you without leaving better and happier.

Mother Teresa

As nurses we are trained to be aware of not only people, but circumstances, so we can make good assessments with great outcomes.

This one all started when I promised my family I would have another garage sale so we could trade our trash for cash. Included in the sale were some "interesting" flowered draperies that my son had taken off the windows of his newly purchased town home. During the heat of the sale I heard a woman exclaim to her husband, "Oh, what lovely draperies!" I immediately was drawn to this lady.

"We are missionaries just back from Thailand, and we don't have any drapes on our windows. The padding on the back of these would keep out the cold." Her sweet spirit was so apparent as she looked at the drapes. I told her she could have them for half price. Thrilled, she gathered them up with a lovely smile of gratitude, and left with her husband.

The next day as I was putting leftover items into boxes to donate, I saw the missionary husband coming up the driveway with a young teenager. The boy was a handsome young man who greeted us with a smile and warm hello, revealing an obvious cleft palate.

The older man explained that he had seen a golf bag the day before that he thought his adopted son from Bulgaria would love. The young man said he worked as a golf caddy at a local golf course. His eyes lit up as he explored the bag closely. "How much is it?" he asked.

"Three dollars," his dad answered as he read the sticker. The young man then asked his dad if he could have his allowance early, to which his dad agreed, pulling out three one-dollar bills. The youngster started to hand me the three dollars when I clasped his hand and said, "Just keep it and get yourself something else."

His expression turned to joy as he started down our driveway, almost dancing and with a huge smile on his face. He repeated, "Thank you, lady, thank you so much!"

I called out to him, "You can have anything else you want before we pack up!"

The father also called out to his son, "Rosen! Rosen!" then repeated my offer, but the boy didn't hear either of us. His dad sighed and smiled broadly, explaining that his son was so overjoyed with the new golf bag that he couldn't think about anything else.

It really struck me how genuinely grateful this young man was for something as simple as a used golf bag. He was content with what he had received, and desired nothing else.

That night as I lay in bed I kept thinking about how grateful Rosen had been. God seemed to whisper in my ear how much he loved the people who serve Him so unselfishly and expect little in return—like this missionary family. I drifted off to sleep thinking about how great it would be if Rosen had his mouth fixed.

My thoughts continued as I visited my dentist, Dr. Kyle Edlund, the next week. I told him the garage sale story and asked him if he had ever partnered in helping out people with limited resources. He looked at me intently, paused for just a moment, and then said with a smile, "If you can find him, I will treat him."

My heart leapt with joy thinking of how this young teenager's self-esteem and future could be impacted.

I contacted the caddy master at the golf course asking if he had a caddy there with a cleft palate. The man acted very protective, asking why I wanted to know. I told him the garage sale story and how a few of us felt led to help this young man. The manager softened immediately as he affirmed what a beautiful thing that would be. He shared that Rosen had been named "Caddy of the Year" that past year because of his excellent attitude going that extra mile in service to others.

When I called Rosen's number, his adopted mother answered. I told her I was the "garage-sale drape lady," and explained our plan to help repair Rosen's cleft palate. She had tears in her voice as she shared that the timing was certainly the Lord's. Two days earlier Rosen had had three teeth pulled at a university hospital where students get experience by performing procedures, at no charge, for people with lower incomes. The university had called about three hours after the surgery saying they had pulled a wrong tooth and wanted Rosen to come back so they could try to put it back in. The tooth was reinserted, but Rosen was so discouraged and in so much pain that he said he had decided to trust God with his mouth instead of dentists! She went on to explain that he had been an orphan until the age of twelve when they adopted him.

Ostracized because of his facial deformity, he had eaten only rice a couple of times a day and occasionally ate birds to survive. It took a little encouragement, but Rosen agreed to see Dr. Edlund.

My generous dentist not only examined, cleaned, and x-rayed Rosen's teeth, but also consulted with an orthodontist and an oral surgeon. Before Christmas that year, Rosen not only had his cleft palate repaired, but received a full set of braces along with ongoing care from true professionals.

Today Rosen is with Youth with a Mission in a ministry to help street children.

With the help of others, my initial nursing assessment resulted in a great outcome!

Kathy Brown

6

LESSONS

Have you learned the lessons only of those who admired you, and were tender with you, and stood aside for you? Have you not learned great lessons from those who braced themselves against you, and disputed passage with you?

Walt Whitman

The Creepy Visitor

*J*udge not, that you be not judged.

Matthew 7:1

A chill ran up my spine as I sensed his presence. He was lurking in the shadows, near the medicine cart. In an instant, the giant of a man was looming over me.

Tattoos covered his shaved head. A skull inked on his skull had a snake slithering from the eye socket. Skeletons, swords, and scrolls covered every inch of his scalp. He wore a black T-shirt and jeans and boots draped in clanging chains. Fear gripped me as I realized I was alone, trapped inside the dimly lit nurses' station.

In my best authoritarian voice I asked, "May I help you?"

The man straightened up and said, "Yes, Ma'am, I'm Billy. The hospital people said they sent my mother here. They said there is nothing else they can do for her. I know it's late but I've got to see her."

I hoped he didn't notice the obvious relief on my face or my shaky hand as I pointed to his mother's room.

The next night he was back, with a seven-year-old boy in tow. His son had a lightning bolt etched into his hair. The kid wore black clothes and combat boots with silver chains on them. *Oh great,* I thought, *another generation of freaks.*

The boy balked in the doorway and stared at all the medical equipment. He scrunched up his nose at the faint, but unmistakable, odor of death. The man gave his son a little nudge but the child hid behind his father and would not budge. The huge man stooped down to eye level and held the boy by the shoulders. "You're not going to let a bunch of stupid wires and tubes scare you away from seeing your grandma, are you?" he challenged.

The little boy stood solemnly, then wiped his face on his sleeve, puffed out his chest, and strode across the threshold. His grandmother patted a spot next to her and he tentatively climbed up on her bed. Within seconds they were snuggling and giggling.

In the weeks that followed, the child became accustomed to being around sick people. His father reminded him to say "Excuse me," whenever he walked in front of the other patient's TV set. He showed him how to get ice for the grandmother. The kid loved the clatter of the ice going down the chute and refilled her cup every chance he got.

One day the boy passed the therapy room and wanted to know why they were making Grandma's roommate work so hard. His father explained that P.T. (physical therapy) was like P.E. (physical education). The dad asked, "You know that it can be real hard, but it makes you stronger, right?"

"Right!" said the boy, flexing his imaginary muscles.

After that, whenever the patient's roommate returned from therapy, the youngster said, "Good job!"

"How come old Miss Mary gets to go to P.T. and

Grandma always has to take naps?" the boy asked his father. Billy couldn't tell his son that Grandma, who was only in her late forties, was dying and that old Miss Mary was getting better.

Miss Mary, who had outlived her family and friends, began looking forward to their visits. She saved gelatin cups and graham crackers from her lunch tray for the little visitor.

Over the next six weeks, the strange appearance of the father and son faded from my mind. I only saw two people who were making two of my patients' last days worth living.

Billy's biggest fear was that his mother would die alone. He told me to call him when the end was near so he could be with her. I warned him, "Only God knows exactly when someone is going to die; we can't always predict it." But I promised to call immediately if I saw any indications.

The evening came when I had to make that call. His mother's breathing had suddenly become labored. "I'm sorry, but it looks like the end is near," I told him.

He choked out, "I'm coming. Tell her to hang on, I'm coming."

When I returned to her room, she was fading much faster than expected.

"Billy is on his way. He is just down the street; he will be here in a few minutes. Hang on," I pleaded.

Even though she had been comatose for days, I knew she heard me. Her furrowed brow softened and her ragged breathing eased.

Moments later, Billy ran down the hallway and into my waiting arms. I braced the pale, shaken, hulk of a man as we entered the room. He held one of her hands and I held the other. As we waited, he reached over and held my hand too. She stopped struggling for breath the moment he arrived. Her breathing simply became slower and slower . . . until it finally stopped altogether. Billy and I

hugged each other. Then we quickly turned away so neither could see the other crying.

We never saw each other again.

Today I still occasionally judge a book by its cover, but
now I keep on reading until I get to the heart of the story.

Joyce Seabolt

Janet

Time cools, time clarifies; no mood can be maintained quite unaltered through the course of hours.

Mark Twain

"Dave, Channel 9 News is in the lobby," the hospital receptionist called to inform me, rather matter-of-factly. I grabbed a pen and small notepad and bolted out of my office.

This is it! I told myself, as I made my way down the hospital hall and into the elevator. Just one week on the job, this was my first real encounter with the press. It was 1988 and at twenty-three years old, I was one of the youngest people ever hired as press liaison for the city's level-one trauma center, Denver General Hospital. My heart was pounding.

What could it be? I asked myself. *A stabbing, shooting, or multicar accident? Maybe it's a hostage situation and the SWAT team has taken out some crazed lunatic.*

Either way, I was to assess the situation, gather the

pertinent information, glean the relevant facts, and disseminate them to the news media in the most cohesive, articulate, and professional manner. *Take a deep breath, Buddy. It's showtime.*

As the elevator doors opened, I stepped into the hospital lobby and was taken aback. Instead of a television camera and a reporter, there was a large group of people milling about in the hospital lobby, many wearing the "9 News" insignia. Speaking in hushed tones, there was concern on their faces as they hugged and consoled each other.

I approached a young woman in the group, identified myself as the public relations representative of the hospital, and asked if I could be of assistance.

"Yes please," she implored. "Our friend and coworker was just in a bad accident and we just need to know how she is."

Clearly needing to just talk to someone, she told me of this wonderful woman named Sandy who was one of the best-loved administrative assistants at the news station. An older woman and longtime married, Sandy was going on a rare "girls only" vacation with her best friends. As she drove to the airport, she was in a terrible accident and was badly injured.

As the minutes passed, the crowd of concerned supporters grew until the lobby was overflowing with friends, family, and other 9 News staffers.

"We're just so worried about her," one said through her tears. "We just haven't heard anything for a while and I wonder if you could get us some kind of update."

"Let me go check and see where things are," I told her, not really knowing what to do or even who to ask—I was so new on the job. Most of my time had been spent learning about the hospital and preparing for news media encounters—but not like this one.

As the major trauma center, Denver General (DG) had

long been known as the "Knife and Gun Club." Significant injuries were not uncommon at DG—nor were the crowds of worried families and friends. But all of this was new to me. Moreover, it was about 4:15 PM on a Friday afternoon. Many others had gone home for the weekend and there was no one to turn to for guidance.

What is my role here, if any? I asked myself. Was my job at DG merely to act as liaison for news stories about injured patients? Was it to act as hospital spokesman in times of crisis or public inquiry?

Here was a lobby filled with despondent, anxious people—many of them with very familiar faces—yet I was at a loss. It was Friday night. I was single and had planned to meet up with some friends. *What am I supposed to do?*

I decided that, with no direction available, all I could do was what I could. So I stayed.

As I turned to make my way to the double doors leading to the operating room, a nurse approached the group and was met with silence as the group surrounded her. "I know how concerned you all are," began Janet. "Sandy was hurt very, very badly. She is in the operating room right now and just know that the doctors are doing all they can. Please be patient and we'll give you updates as soon as we know anything more."

With that she turned away. The group turned in on itself, drawing strength from each other.

Over the next several hours I made shuttle trips to the cafeteria to get food to the group, and acted as a "gopher" for anything else they needed. As the lone house-phone was constantly in use, I gave the very large group access to an adjacent office to make phone calls, as this was in the days prior to cell phones. Mostly, I did what I could.

As the evening wore on, the hourly updates from Janet became more frequent. Late in the evening, Janet returned with an always professional, but more concerned demeanor.

"I have to be honest," she began. "The doctors are having a very difficult time. The injuries are very serious, but she is fighting hard. The doctors have commented several times how amazed they are at her will and her spirit." That comment was met with smiles and nods from her supporters. "She wants to live," Janet continued, "but the injuries are very, very serious. I'll be back soon with some more information."

As she turned to leave, I followed her into the holding area outside the OR and asked what I could do to help.

"Just be there to provide whatever they need," she said, looking me straight in the eyes. "The next hour is going to be very busy and very challenging for them."

The following hour was marked by more frequent visits by Janet, each reporting more grave news than the next.

"She's fighting hard, but the doctors are struggling to stay ahead of her injuries."

"Sandy has an incredible will to live, but there is only so much the doctors can do."

"They are holding out hope, but the odds are against her."

Finally, as 11:00 PM neared, Janet approached the weary group and said with tender compassion, "Sandy has lost her fight."

Drained, the group quietly began embracing each other and turned to Sandy's husband to offer support.

Feeling a bit like an intruder and out of place, I walked back to the OR with Janet and commented on how long Sandy had held on.

"Actually," Janet said quietly as we walked, "she died over an hour ago." Responding to the obviously confused look on my face, she continued.

"An hour ago, her friends and family still had great hope and weren't ready to hear the news. Sandy had fought hard with an incredible spirit, but had I told them so quickly that she had passed, they would have been in shock and would never have heard those words about her wonderful spirit. The last hour was preparing them, emotionally and psychologically, for the news that they would have to hear. But now they know and understand everything that we did and everything that Sandy did to fight. The ending is the same, but they deserved to hear more than the simple, cruel fact that she died."

Despite their profound grief, so many took time to thank me for my help, though I was reluctant to accept their gratitude. I had the easiest job that night—the surgeons had the hardest.

But it was a remarkable nurse named Janet who had the greatest impact on Sandy's "family," and on me. She was Sandy's voice, to help all who loved her understand.

David Avrin

A Lesson in Saying Good-bye

Love one human being purely and warmly and you will love all.

Jean Paul Richter

As I sat with my father during his final days, my mind sometimes wandered to years gone by. One afternoon my thoughts drifted back to my sixteenth year, when the mother of my future husband was dying from breast cancer. When she told me, "I'm dying," all I could manage to reply was, "I know." I was young and inexperienced and felt terribly inadequate.

But now, after more than twenty years of nursing, I've learned that there are many ways of dealing with death. One death in particular affected me tremendously.

On that memorable day, Terri, the night nurse, told me in report that Paddy Doyle had been admitted the previous evening. A spirited elderly man, Paddy had been a patient many times in the past. He was as jolly as Santa Claus, and we'd all grown fond of him.

But this time he was dying.

Terri said, "His wife went home 'to refresh' late last evening. She left strict instructions to be called if his status changed. Did you know they just celebrated their sixtieth wedding anniversary? It's so sad.

"Paddy's feet are dusky and he's been slipping in and out of consciousness for the last hour. I called his wife and she's on her way."

The words were barely out of her mouth when Mrs. Doyle glided down the hallway, looking so elegant that I could hardly believe she'd been a bride sixty years ago. She looked as though she'd had her hair coiffed at the beauty parlor and her makeup was flawless. I doubted that she'd slept a wink getting ready for her final date with her husband.

She took the news of his impending death in a dignified way. Squaring her narrow shoulders, she made her way to his room, her feet barely making a sound on the polished floor.

Being young, I didn't want to consider that someday I might have to go through the same thing with my own husband. I wanted to cry for her loss. They hadn't had children, and most of their relatives were old and sick. How was she going to adjust to being alone?

On my rounds to assess patients, I paused outside of Paddy's closed door. I didn't know what to say to this couple, who were like grandparents to me.

I knocked lightly on the door but got no answer. As I started to walk away, the door slowly opened.

"Come in, child," said Mrs. Doyle graciously, stepping back from the door.

He looks awful, I thought as I approached my patient. *Why is this so hard? I wish I'd called in sick.*

I immediately regretted my sentiments. *Better get your act together. She's going to need you.*

Then I noticed that she didn't need me. In fact, she was holding up quite well.

Mrs. Doyle resumed her business and seemed unaware of my presence. She spoke to her husband softly, saying, "I'm going to get you cleaned up, Paddy."

"Do you need help?" I asked.

"No dear. We can manage." With that, she moved to the sink to fill a basin with water.

I listened while she told him, "I'm going to wash your face now." He muttered something unintelligible. I don't know how she understood what he said, but she did. Locks of his white hair had fallen across his brow. As she swept the strands back, she murmured, "There they go again." I realized I'd witnessed an intimate moment that had been repeated for sixty years.

With her fingertips, she lightly caressed the back of his hand, then scooped his hand into hers. "There now," she said. He gave her hand a barely perceptible squeeze.

I suddenly noticed that the air was filled with cologne. After all the time I'd spent caring for Paddy, I'd never noticed his scent before.

Paddy stirred.

"Hush, I'm right here." Mrs. Doyle sat on the edge of the bed. She gazed into his clouded blue eyes. "It's okay. I won't leave."

That was it. I started looking for the exit. It was breaking my heart to watch them on this day, their last together. Of course she wasn't going to leave him, but I could.

Hesitating by the door, I wondered, *How is she doing it? I'd be crying and screaming mad at the whole world.*

Mrs. Doyle reached into her pocket and withdrew her rosary. She began to pray.

Clutching my necklace cross for strength, I prayed too. *God, let this be over for Paddy. Please don't make him suffer any longer.*

As I held tight to my cross and closed my eyes,

something strange happened—I felt the presence of someone else in the room. Opening my eyes, I saw only the elderly couple. I closed my eyes and felt it again. Someone or
something else was there.

I opened my eyes and saw a young couple, lovers, gazing into each other's eyes. Two people meeting and falling
in love and laughing. I could feel the joy inside the sorrow.
A feeling of peace came over me.

I'd found what I'd desperately needed. I walked over to
the bed and gave Mrs. Doyle a hug. I held Paddy's hand
and told him, "I'm going to miss your smile."

Then I left the room. This was their time to say good-bye.

My father stirred as I held his hand. I said, "Hush Dad,
I'm right here. I won't leave you."

Barbara Scales
as previously published in Nursing ©2005

One Patient

*Hear my prayer, O God; give ear to the words of
my mouth.*

Psalms 54:2

I often review this episode in my mind. Little did I realize at the time that one patient would have such an impact
on me.

She was an eighty-seven-year-old woman, who I'll refer
to as Mrs. G. She was transported from the local nursing
home with an acute inferior wall myocardial infarction.
Until a year ago, she lived with her family, who said that,
although she was physically weak, she remained "sharp as
a tack." Presently, she was in acute pulmonary edema and
hypotensive with an unstable cardiac rhythm. I remember
how frightened she looked as she lay there surrounded by
two nurses, three physicians, and a respiratory therapist.
Within minutes she had a tube placed in her mouth,
another in her nose, and a catheter inserted into her right
neck, and both hands firmly restrained at her side.

Her "periods of agitation" were noted by everyone in

the room. Even though both hands were snuggly restrained, she continued to pull and thrash in bed. It became obvious to me that she became more agitated each time I entered the room, and I said a silent prayer that no one else noted my effect on her. I wondered if she thought I was the one who had intubated her, or if the restraint I applied was too tight. I spoke to her often and she seemed alert, nodding appropriately to the questions I asked her.

Before long, Mrs G.'s condition started to deteriorate; medications were started and titrated as we closely monitored her progress. In spite of this, she followed me with her eyes, pointed to me with her restrained hands, and continued trying to speak. The pulmonologist insisted she was becoming more restless and confused secondary to hypoxia and should be sedated to avoid self-extubation.

At this time I was alone with her and stood by her side. "What is it you are trying to tell me?"

I untied her right hand and, still holding it firmly, placed a pen in it. I held a paper and watched this aged woman trembling, determined to write something she obviously felt was important.

After she wrote three words, her head fell back on the pillow and her hands relaxed. I restrained her again, although for the first time I felt no resistance.

I looked at the paper and saw the words she was so desperate to write, so large they covered the entire page: "God bless you."

Peggy Krepp

There Is Nun Better

For health and the constant enjoyment of life, give me a keen and ever-present sense of humor; it is the next best thing to an abiding faith in providence.

George B. Cheever

Sister Catherine Higley, a Benedictine nun, was my colleague, friend, and teammate at the hospice. As a nurse, she was a blessing to many and she and I had wonderful times caring for people at the end of their lives. She had such a balanced view of life and death, and her wisdom was a great support to me.

Sister Catherine had the ability to give it to you straight while showing an extraordinary amount of compassion at the same time. One of her patients referred to her as Attila the Nun! Yet he lovingly followed her every command because he knew that she cared for him and he deeply respected her.

Once she was working with Mr. Johnson who was terminally ill. I was the social worker assigned to the case. I called his wife to schedule my first visit. We set up a time and just before she hung up the phone, she said, "Can you save my husband?"

I didn't know if she meant save him physically or spiritually, so, in my zealous intent to do the right thing, I said, "How do you mean?" (You must realize that "how do you mean?" comes from two years of intensive graduate study in the art and science of social work culminating with the perfect question to elicit just the right response from the client!)

She said, "Can you save his faith?"

I immediately knew that this was a job for the chaplain, so I explained to Mrs. Johnson that I would have the chaplain follow up with her as soon as possible.

The next day, I was approached by "Attila" in the hallway at the hospice office. She was furious. "I can't believe you're sending the chaplain to Mr. Johnson's house. They said from the very beginning that they wanted nothing to do with chaplains and you know we respect that!"

"That's odd," I said, "I just spoke to Mrs. Johnson yesterday and she said she wanted someone to save her husband's faith."

"No she didn't," Sister Catherine retorted, "She wanted someone to 'shave his face.' And she's very confused as to why the chaplain has to do that!"

Thanks to Attila the Nun, I headed off the chaplain and avoided a very close shave!

Ronald P. Culberson

Fish Therapy

The most wasted of all days is one without laughter.

e. e. cummings

Several years ago I had the pleasure of lounging around as a hospital patient for several days as the result of a staph infection. My profession was in health care and in fact I worked at this facility, so I knew many of the hospital staff well. Although it was a serious infection, I did not feel sick per se, and found myself on the receiving end of a few minor practical jokes, which of course were totally undeserved. (I swear I have no idea how the door to the supply cabinet in my room got stuck shut with a dozen strips of heavy-duty, two-sided tape hidden on the inside cabinet doorjamb.)

I awoke the second day of my stay when a nurse came in to change my IV fluids, which included several differing bags of solutions and antibiotics. I noticed immediately that she was carrying a large, old-fashioned glass bottle of fluid—at least a liter in size.

That's odd, I thought.

Then I saw the three goldfish circling happily in the water. I spotted my friend Gary, the pharmacist, lurking nearby, and he, the nurse, and I laughed and carried on about my fish. For some reason, it just seemed right to name the three fish Larry, Moe, and Curly Gary, which was a slight misnomer since Gary was a few hairs shy of curly.

They started to take the fish away, but seeing opportunity rear its mischievous face, I asked them to wait a bit.

"Don't tell the nurses on the next shift about the fish," I suggested.

It's amazing how easy it is to enlist silent coconspirators. I turned the bottle spout up and uncorked it so the fish could breathe until the afternoon.

As the 3:30 shift change approached, I recorked the goldfish bottle and hung it behind the largest of my IV bags so the fish were mostly out of sight. I then carefully taped extra tubing from the fish bottle to my IV line so that there appeared to be a connection.

Just after the shift change, I pressed the call button. "My IV has a problem."

The lambs are always the first to be slaughtered, so a newly hired nurse who was recently out of school was dispatched to my room to check the IV.

As she entered the room, she asked, "Your IV has a problem?"

"I hate to harp, but I think maybe the IV line is blocked."

She started checking the IV site at my wrist, as most nurses are trained to do. Seeing no problem, she traced the line upward, checking each connection. As she got halfway up multiple tubes, the movement of one of the fish caught her eye. She shrieked so loudly that I jumped even higher than she did, which must have been impressive considering both the height of her leap and that I was lying flat on my back. I am sure even the fish jumped.

When she landed, she covered her mouth with both hands and shouted, "Oh my God, oh my God!"

The laughter of her coworkers filled the doorway behind her. She turned toward them, fanning her face with her hand.

"Man," I said, "you scared the bejeebers out of me! That's no way to treat a patient!"

"Out of *you*!" she said breathlessly. "You should have been in my shoes!"

"Are they still on?" I smirked

I had high hopes for the next shift change, but that nurse simply came in, gave me a "You-are-so-busted, Mister" look, shook her head, and went about her business.

The next day, Larry, Moe, and Curly Gary were discharged and sent home to live happy goldfish lives as pets of one of the nurses' children. The day after that, as I was saying a fond farewell to my hospital "gown" and preparing to go home, a patient from the adjacent room stopped at the doorway of my room and said, "You know, I've been in the hospital a lot recently, but this was absolutely my best hospitalization."

"Why is that?" I asked.

"Because laughter is good medicine."

"Laughter *is* good medicine," I chuckled. "Nurses and patients need a dose more often."

Daniel James

Bridge to a Silent World

The words that enlighten the soul are more precious than jewels.

Hazrat Inayat Khan

As a nurse health educator, I've had many rewarding opportunities, from being a professor of nursing at a community college, to teaching health classes for the hearing-impaired children in an elementary school. The latter led me to teach sign language to the parents of a six-year-old.

On the day I first met her, the afternoon still held on to the sunlight. Inside the wood-frame home, shadows clung in the small kitchen where I sat with Michele and her mother, Carolyn. Michele, a student in the School for the Deaf in Great Falls, Montana, was on a home visit. Huge brown eyes spoke her confusion. The beauty of her delicate features was marred with sadness.

Over a cup of coffee, I explained the home-signing program to Carolyn. Michele sat on the floor in a corner with a few scattered toys. When she got up, jerky movements hampered her walking. Her hand clutched a string to a toy she pulled on wheels; a clown with a kitten tucked under its arm. Halfway across the room, Michele stumbled and sprawled across the coffee table, knocking several items to the floor.

Her mother frowned, shook her head, and gave an abrupt hand motion to wave her away. Her sharp words were cloaked with irritation as she pointed to a small chair in the corner. "Go sit there!" she said, knowing her daughter couldn't hear her.

Mirroring her mother's frown, Michele signed. "Why I go?"

Confusion swept across her mother's face. "Don't sass me!" She pushed Michele toward the corner chair. Sniffles accompanied Michele's unsteady gait.

My spirits tumbled. "She was signing to you. Asking, 'Why I go?'" I explained.

"Well, I didn't know that. It looked like she was making fun of me. She's always misbehaving. It's difficult for everyone when she's home."

I knew of the pain parents felt. I worked with other parents who shared the guilt and blame they experienced having a hearing-impaired child.

"I think you'll find it easier to have Michele at home when you understand what she's signing to you," I offered. "You'll be amazed at the difference in her behavior after you've learned even a few signs."

I told Carolyn about the school support program. We marked her calendar with a schedule for my visits. Occasionally I paused to smile at Michele who watched from her chair a few feet away. I gave Carolyn a book with signs and went over a few sample lessons. I expressed the importance of her husband learning to sign with her and suggested they practice together.

I answered Carolyn's last question and turned to Michele. I gazed at her puzzled expression, wondering what she was thinking. A blue barrette barely hung on to her short black hair. Slowly, I signed . . . "My name is Peg. I'm your new friend. I'm going to help your mother and father learn sign language."

Michele raised her slender arms, bent her small fingers, and signed, "My name . . ." she made an M and touched the dimple in her right cheek. But her dimple disappeared when she made the sign for mother.

Before I left, I helped Carolyn sign her first sentences to Michele. "You were a good girl while I talked with Peg. Thank you."

Then to Michele I signed, "Have fun at school. I'll see you when you come home for Christmas."

She smiled and waved good-bye.

All that fall, I met with Carolyn twice a week. Whenever I asked about her husband joining our signing lessons, the reply was the same. "He's too busy."

"Tell your husband that children look to Dad as well as Mom for answers to their questions and support for their fears. 'Where do the sun and moon come from? What are stars? Why do others make fun of me? I'm scared in the dark.' Explain to him that when a parent ignores their child's questions, their thought is, 'Why doesn't Daddy love me?'"

At my next visit Carolyn said, "My husband told me waving his hands makes him feel silly. He talks to her by pointing to things."

"Everyone feels a little awkward at the beginning," I said. "Pointing is a fun game for children. But ask him how will he feel when Michele is older and ignores his pointing when she signs?"

At our next lesson, Michele's father sat at the kitchen table. He listened intently and began to slowly repeat simple signs. During my weekly visits, I watched as this family's emotional scars began to heal.

When Michele was home for Christmas vacation, I was invited for coffee one afternoon. When I stepped into the house, pine scent mingled with the aroma of perking coffee. Michele took my hand and led me to the Christmas tree decorated with tinsel, colored glass balls, wooden beads, and small blinking lights. She pointed to a paper angel on the top of the tree. "I made for Mother and Dad," she signed.

"It's beautiful, Michele."

Her dimple appeared with a wide grin.

"Ask Peg if she wants a cookie," Carolyn signed.

"Mom is learning to sign with me," Michele signed and beamed a smile. "Sometimes Dad tries and my little brother knows some words with his hands." She giggled. "When his fingers look funny, I help him."

"I'm happy for all of you," I signed.

When I left that day, mother and daughter held hands while waving good-bye.

A year later, my program with Michele's parents was finished. I planned my last visit to say good-bye when Michele was home at Thanksgiving.

"Mom and Dad's signing lessons with me are all done," I signed. "I won't be coming anymore . . . "

"But you're my friend. Who will help Mother and Dad?" Michele signed. Tears welled in her beautiful brown eyes.

"You can be their teacher now."

Carolyn signed. "Yes, we need your help."

Michele smiled and hugged her mother.

"I'll come by to see you when you are home at Christmastime."

"I love you," she signed.

"I love you too," I signed.

As I opened the door to leave, snowflakes drifted, leaving a dusting of snow over the stately pine trees grouped in their front yard. I thanked Michelle again for the plate of Christmas cookies she and her mother made for me and her dimple deepened. I looked back at their room dressed for the Christmas season. *This year,* I thought, *Carolyn and her husband opened the best present of all. Speech.*

A loving bridge to their daughter's silent world.

Margaret Hevel

The Survivor

Be kind, for everyone you meet is fighting a hard battle.

Plato

It had always been difficult for me to watch old men cry. Helpless and unsure, I couldn't imagine the hardships they endured in life . . . the want of the Depression to the horrors of world wars. When they cried, they wept for their parents trying to put food on the table, for friends lost, for themselves.

About eleven years ago I cared for a gentleman who had had a severe stroke, and it was hard to understand him when he talked. But he couldn't talk anyway because he just kept crying.

"Are you having a lot of pain?" I'd ask. He always shook his head no.

"What can I do for you?"

"Nothing," he would answer. Then he'd look at me as his eyes filled with tears.

I offered, "Let me know if there's anything I can do for you."

The old man would nod his head, then tears spilled down his face until both cheeks were drenched. Since he couldn't wipe his own eyes, I would dab a tissue on his sodden cheeks, then leave, wondering what was really hurting him.

One day, the old man's son came to visit. He approached me and asked how his father was doing. I told him that I didn't know if his father was sad because of his stroke or if something else was bothering him.

"Let me see if I can figure it out," the son said. "I've got a good idea of what it is."

About a half hour later, he came to me. "My dad was a survivor of the USS *Indianapolis*. They were on a secret mission at the end of World War II. They were struck by torpedoes and sunk. No one knew they were there because they had no radio contact. For five days they were in the water while sharks circled around them and picked off people one by one."

"How horrible!"

"It was. My dad has never cried about it. He said that since he's been lying in bed, that's all he can think about."

With this information, I knew what I had to do to care for him. I pulled up a chair when he started talking and just let him talk. I learned to accustom my ear to the old man's speech pattern and he told me the whole incredible story. He spoke of the sounds in the water when the sharks came and the screams as hundreds of men were yanked under. He spoke of the frigid water on his body and the darkness at night.

"It was so dark you couldn't see the person next to you," he wept. "We kept talking at night so we wouldn't feel so alone. We were all afraid to go to sleep. But the worst part was the never-ending thirst."

I choked back tears. "I'm always amazed at what people can endure."

He smiled in that gentle way of his. "I wonder if the reason I keep thinking about it is to give me the strength to come back from my stroke." He paused for a few seconds. "Because this is the hardest battle I've ever fought. But if I made it through the *Indianapolis,* I can make it through this too."

And he did.

From that day on he worked diligently at his physical therapy and became . . . again . . . a survivor.

Mary Clare Lockman

This Is Bill

How far you go in life depends on your being tender with the young, compassionate with the aged, sympathetic with the striving, and tolerant of the weak and the strong—because someday you will have been all of these.

George Washington Carver

It was one of those days in the nursing profession that you just have to get through. The workload was heavy, the pace frenetic. Everybody wanted something from me, and they all seemed to want it at the same time. As I hurriedly finished my lunch, in my mind I organized the tasks I needed to complete that afternoon. It was going to be a tight fit, but I thought I could get everything done.

But as soon as I returned to the floor, things began to unravel.

I got a report on an unexpected admission from one of my coworkers: "They brought some old guy up from the unit to die." Without waiting for further explanation, I headed toward what had been my only empty bed. It was now occupied by an elderly gentleman, and as I entered the room I knew that he had already done what he had been sent there to do. Without fanfare, without attendance, without anyone even knowing it, this person had left the world.

I was filled with righteous indignation, as I made my way back to the nurses' station to start the long and time-consuming process that surrounds a death in the hospital. For me it had always been important to see that someone was with my patients as they died. As a matter of principle, I felt that we had failed this man. How could the nurses from the ICU let his family go home when his death was so imminent? Why had he been dropped on my doorstep in the last few minutes of his life? And where was his family, anyway? As the questions whirred through my mind, anger rose in me like bitter bile. I was mad at everybody, including the poor old man who had died so unceremoniously on my watch.

Unable to reach anyone at the phone number listed under next of kin, I called the designated funeral home and went back to his room to try to garner some information from his meager personal effects.

Stacked in the corner in standard-issue hospital plastic bags were his belongings: a worn pair of work boots, a cap embroidered with a local feed company's logo, a faded pair of bib overalls. In one of the pockets I found a wallet but no driver's license or other identification. My frustration mounted. As I started to stuff it back into the pocket I saw a piece of yellow paper peeking out from one of the sections. I opened it and began to read. It was written with big block letters and had the telltale look of a palsied hand.

"Well, honey," it said, "if you are reading this, it probably means that things didn't go so good for me this time. I know you did everything you could." It went on for a while, sharing some memories. At the end it was signed simply "Love, Bill." Tears of shame and sorrow filled my eyes as I realized that this letter was to me and my coworkers. Indeed, I had just lost an old friend.

Bill was everybody's friend. He had no real family, just one cousin in a distant state. He had outlived the rest of his family and his contemporaries. For the past several years he had been fighting the demons of old age. Repeated hospital visits brought him to the floor where I worked. He always came with a crooked smile and a kind word. He came with big floppy old ears that were interested in all that was going on in the world and in others' lives. He came with a simple wisdom and a gentle nature toward his fellow man.

"Did you find out who this guy belongs to?" asked one of my coworkers as he shot past the room to keep pace with his own schedule. When I didn't answer he backtracked and peeked into the room. I stood crying silently and contemplating the face of a man that I knew so well, yet hadn't recognized at all. Swelling, illness, and death had transformed him. The love that he radiated in life had left along with his soul.

"Don't you know who this is?" I asked sadly. "He belongs to us. This is Bill."

He left in silence to spread the word. Soon there was a small army of nurses at the door.

Gently my coworkers helped me with the postmortem cares. We talked about Bill and all that he had meant to us. We remembered the time that he brought us homemade bread. Since he could no longer drive, he carefully coordinated the timing of his baking with the bus schedule so that the bread would arrive still warm. We recalled the time that he brought trinkets to everyone at Christmas, making two trips on the bus in the bitter cold so he could deliver his gifts to each of the shifts personally.

In due time the funeral home attendant arrived and Bill

was transported to the elevator with an honor guard of sorts. Every nurse on duty stopped what they were doing and came to escort our old friend off the floor for the last time.

Soon enough we were all back to the tasks at hand. Our patients were concerned with their own problems. Few were aware that a death had occurred on the unit that day. But on that day Bill taught me something profound and lasting that has guided me throughout my nursing career, and that something is this . . . that everyone is someone's Bill.

In nursing school they taught me about psychology. They taught me about the fight or flight response and about Maslow's hierarchy of needs. They taught me about the different ways people tend to respond to the stress of hospitalization. But nothing in a book or from Freud or Maslow could teach me what Bill did.

There are days in nursing when things don't go well. Sometimes patients don't act in ways that you might expect, and sometimes they don't even act in ways that make much sense. Pain and fear and frustration have chipped away at the core of the person until you can't recognize who they really are. These are the days that I make myself stop and ask a simple question: "Don't you know who this is?" And the answer comes. This is someone who has a life that you don't even know about. This is someone who has hopes and dreams and fears. This is someone who is loved and cherished by people that you haven't even met.

This is Bill.

Susan Stava

The Value of Time

We must use time wisely and forever realize that the time is always ripe to do right.

Nelson Mandela

As a nurse, I knew the battle of the nursing shortage and our inability to spend individual time with our patients. When I flipped to the other side of the bed rail and became a mastectomy patient, I wanted to be as little fuss for the nursing staff as possible.

I arrived on the post-op ward at 3:00 PM with nausea and vomiting. Instead of putting on my call bell, I recruited my family to help measure my emesis. The nursing unit was short-staffed that evening, something I deciphered from hearing nurses talking outside my door. It was cracked open only six inches—but sound travels more than we realize. One nurse had called in sick with no one to cover for her. There were two Whipple (pancreatic surgery) patients who were fresh post-ops. Another patient had crumped (coded) and was taken to the SICU. It was organized chaos.

Myckie, my evening shift nurse, came in every ninety minutes or so to empty my hemovacs, check my I&O, and ask me how I was feeling. I had declined pain medication due to the nausea problem. Each time Myckie prepared to leave my room she would say, "How are you doing?"

I answered, as if rehearsed, "I'm fine." That was the extent of our conversations.

My husband left at 10:00 PM to go home to our child and I was alone for the first time to reflect on what had happened, and to deal with the reality of a cancer diagnosis with still unknown pathology. That would determine the rest of my treatment and potentially my fate.

At 10:50 PM, Myckie reentered my room to empty my drains one more time and record the amount remaining in my IV bag. She again asked, "How are you doing?"

I again responded, "I'm fine."

She paused, put my side rail down, and sat beside me. We made eye contact for the first time. She stared right at me and said, "How *are* you doing?"

I started to cry. "I don't know how I got on the other side of this side rail but it is really scary over here." I told her my worries about my future, about my child, in the event I lost my life to this disease. I rambled for twenty minutes. She didn't utter a word, but held my hand, focusing her eyes on mine and nodding that she was listening intently. It was now 11:10 PM. A unit clerk came to the door and sternly said, "Myckie, you are late for report."

Myckie didn't turn around but kept her focus on me. "Tell them to wait. I'm taking care of a patient."

Myckie gave me that night what she had the least to give . . . her time. I didn't need special sophisticated machines or interpretation of test results. I needed to express myself and know I wasn't alone.

I've read before that we know the value of time when we measure it in ways of what we lost as a result of not having enough of it. A student learns the value of a year when he is held back in grade eight. A mother knows the value of a month when she gives birth to a premature baby. The grandmother, late for a plane for her daughter's wedding, knows the value of an hour.

We nurses know the value of the few moments we are privileged to have being present to our patients.

Lillie D. Shockney

"We should talk about how time constraints prevent us from dealing with the emotional needs of patients, but I have to run."

Reprinted by permission of Aaron Bacall. ©2006 Aaron Bacall.

7

MATTER OF PERSPECTIVE

We ourselves feel that what we are doing is just a drop in the ocean. But the ocean would be less because of that missing drop.

Mother Teresa

Fifty-Fifty

There are truths that are not for all men, nor for all occasions.

Voltaire

As nurses we know that third-degree burns are generally pain free because nerve endings have been destroyed. At the same time, the burned patient is usually alert and conscious, unless they have also sustained a brain injury.

When the rescue crew loaded Mr. E. into the helicopter, he asked what his chances were. The nurse knew he was in serious shape, but not wanting to destroy his hope, he hedged, "I think you have a fifty-fifty chance, my friend."

When Mr. E. arrived at the regional burn center, he was stabilized in the emergency room and the burn surgeon came down to review the resuscitation efforts. The surgeon was a straight-shooting, mustached professional who looked like he could have been a marshal in Dodge City during the days of cowboys and gunfights.

Mr. E. looked up at him and asked, "Doc, what do you think my chances are?"

The doctor looked earnestly at Mr. E. and replied, "Do you want me to be truthful?"

"I'm not sure I have time for you to be anything else," Mr. E. returned.

"I don't think you can survive your burn injuries."

Mr. E. paused for a minute and then replied, "Put me back in the helicopter. I like their odds better."

L. Sue Booth

[EDITORS' NOTE: *Mr. E. holds the record for surviving the highest percentage of burns and for leaving the burn unit successfully. Today, he lives independently in his own home, drives his own car, and is helping to raise his three children. He volunteers to meet with burned victims and their families, and talks to occupational and physical therapy students, nurses, and doctors about the care and psyche of burned patients.*]

A Necessary Change

Look well into thyself; there is a source of strength which will always spring up if thou wilt always look there.

Marcus Aurelius Antoninus

The early morning air powerfully penetrated the multiple layers I was wearing. The cold air stole my breath away. I quickly navigated the three blocks from home to work. As I hurried across the parking lot, I offered a quick, obligatory prayer asking God to help me care for my patients and families.

I finished getting report when the phone rang; my patient's son wanted an update on his dad's condition. I told him of Dick's critical condition, trying my best to sound unhurried. I mentioned that if the family wanted to speak to the doctor, they would need to be here before eight o'clock that morning.

Another glance at my watch, and I hurriedly gathered my patient's chart and headed for his room. *Had I been too matter of fact? Was there compassion in my voice?* I tried to dismiss the knot in my throat. The report I had received on

Dick was grim. Dismissing the urge to pray, I focused my attention on thoroughly assessing him. The clock on the wall taunted me. I was behind my normal schedule. I completed Dick's assessment and basic care, and hurried next door to my next patient.

I had barely begun my assessment when the charge nurse came to inform me that Dick's wife was here. An hour behind. Taking a deep breath, I flung my charting aside and scuttled into Dick's room. A short, blue-eyed, smiling woman greeted me. Her voice was soft like her fluffy white hair.

"Hello, I am Dick's wife, Dianne."

With a halfhearted smile, I gave my customary, "Hi, my name is Anne. I'll be Dick's nurse today."

Before another word was spoken, more of Dick's family walked in. Once again I updated them on his grave condition. I tried patiently to answer all their questions. It was the last comment by Dick's daughter that blindsided me.

"How can you work in the intensive care unit and not go home every night crying?"

Her brown eyes questioned me; her words penetrated my bitter heart. Millions of thoughts darted through my head. I couldn't tell her the truth, it would sound so callous: *after six years in intensive care you get accustomed to death.* Astoundingly, my mouth opened and my heart spoke for me.

"I couldn't do this job without God," I managed to say halfheartedly.

The corners of her lips rose for a brief moment, and then there was silence.

Without taking time to speak another word, I scurried out of the room with a troubled heart. *When had I become so coldhearted? Am I really indifferent to death and suffering?* I needed to talk to someone about this, but I didn't have the time. I had to rid myself of this foreboding darkness pressing in on me.

I returned to the nurses' station. As I sat charting, one of Dick's doctors came into the ICU. I followed him down the hall toward Dick's room.

"It doesn't look good," he muttered to me.

"His family is here to talk to you."

"Nothing has changed. If the pneumonia doesn't kill him, the cancer will. And with his bad heart and kidneys, he doesn't stand a chance."

"His family needs to know that."

The doctor nodded.

I brought Dianne into Dick's room and listened as she talked with the doctor.

My stomach churned as he spoke.

"Unfortunately, there's not much we can do," he said.

After such devastating news, I was astonished to see Dianne's radiant smile. *She is in denial,* I thought.

Dianne stroked her husband's hand.

A tear formed in my eye. *It's been years since I've cried at work. What on earth is happening to me?*

I hustled out to continue my overwhelming assignment. Five hours into my shift the ventilator alarm sounded in Dick's room. I rushed in to determine the cause. After a rapid assessment of Dick and the equipment, I hollered for the charge nurse to call the respiratory therapist. We failed at our endeavor to rectify the situation. Dick continued to struggle for air, even though he was on a respirator. My chest grew tight as I allowed myself to fully experience the severity of the situation. A bedside chest x-ray revealed a pocket of air in his chest, hindering his lung expansion and decreasing the air he received with each breath.

I rushed to the waiting room and ushered Dianne and her family into a small private conference room. I noticed Dianne's eyes filling with tears as I stated plainly Dick's condition.

She whispered, "So this is it?"

Like a melting iceberg, I felt my heart beginning to thaw. I swallowed hard trying to force the tears away. "Would you like to go see him?"

I helped her out of the chair and Dianne and I plodded toward Dick's room. I had walked these halls many times that day, but my feet felt heavy and encumbered. With each step, I felt tremendous sorrow; I began envisioning what it would be like if I had to say good-bye to my husband. My heart beat rapidly in my chest, and my palms began to sweat.

Closing the door behind us, I watched Dianne take a deep breath, stand up tall, and march to the head of Dick's bed. Leaning over she placed a gentle kiss on his forehead, "I love you, Dick. I always have. There won't be a day goes by when I won't miss you or think about you. But now it is time to go see your Savior. Jesus is here, Dick, and it is time for you to run into His arms."

Tears flowed down my cheeks. I walked over to Dianne and put my arm around her. We said a prayer together. At her request, I went out and summoned the rest of the family. They gathered around his bed, and with heads bowed and tears flowing, they gave Dick back to his Lord.

As I helped Dianne and her family cope with the loss of their beloved, I experienced a revival in my spirit. Jesus forgave my indifference and renewed the compassion I needed to care for my patients and their families.

That night on my walk home I cried ... for what Dianne lost ... and I gained.

Anne Johnson

Catch of the Day

Laughter is higher than all pain.

Elbert Hubbard

A phone call.

A plane ride.

A race to the hospital.

I still shuddered at the thought. I had come so close to losing Kyle. Although he wasn't out of the woods yet, at least he was stabilized. At least he was still alive.

In the meantime, my life settled into a routine of its own. A simple breakfast, a ninety-minute drive, and each day spent visiting the care unit to spend time with my twenty-two-year-old son—before the long drive home at night.

During the coma, pneumonia attacked his lungs, infections invaded his blood, and bedsores appeared in odd places. On the other hand, while he was asleep, his cracked ribs healed, his lungs reinflated, and his crushed leg accepted the titanium rod. Now that he was awake and alert, I fretted over the "wait-and-see" outcome of his severe head trauma.

Early on, I had hardly recognized my son. Kyle was like a voodoo doll. Needles, wires, and catheters pierced him. Hoses shackled him. Tubes and cords crisscrossed his body like a fishing net. And it felt odd to see him prone, horizontal, still.

Before this hit-and-run biking accident, nothing about Kyle was still. He was as lively as one of the trout on his stringer—busy flipping and flopping between one activity and the next. Fishing was only one of his outdoor hobbies, like archery and camping. He roamed the foothills of Colorado's Front Range and hunted the Rockies for signs of elk and deer, hoping for a glimpse of moose. And, of course, he tossed the occasional line into icy mountain rivers, looking for relaxation along with a mess of fish to cook over his campfire for supper.

Nevertheless, he was handling his hospitalization better than I was. Those first tenuous hours had melted into days and the days into weeks. Dark circles ringed my eyes, worry lines gridded my forehead, and clothes hung on my too-thin frame. I was exhausted. Utterly worn down. Kyle noticed, I could tell. Now *he* was worrying about *me*.

But today was different.

Even before the elevator doors slid fully open, I heard it. Laughter. *Laughter*?

Oh, it wasn't the stilted laughter of awkward visitors. It wasn't even the brittle laughter born of tension. It was *real* laughter. From the belly. And it was coming from Kyle's room.

I paused at the threshold, hardly believing my ears . . . and eyes. The room pulsed with more than the beeps of monitors. It throbbed with the life that only laughter brings. And it was due to Liam, a new nurse.

His was a one-man comedy routine. He cast out snappy jokes, witty one-liners, and rib-tickling stories. Not only was Kyle actually grinning, so was the small crowd of staff that had collected to provide an avid audience and to egg Liam on—while he reeled in everyone with his nonsense.

My initial reaction was indignation. *How dare he? Didn't this cocky male nurse know the seriousness of Kyle's condition? Didn't he understand how to act in a hospital room?*

As I paused in frustration, I looked toward my son—and witnessed a slow smile spread across his face. It widenened until it erupted into a full-fledged grin. His golden eyes were bright as they met mine. I could see his own quick wit itching to toss out a few quips of his own. I knew that, if it weren't for the trach at the base of his throat, he would be matching Liam, joke for joke. Suddenly, for the first time in weeks, my own spirits lightened and lifted . . . with hope.

I, too, found myself responding to the gags and tales. It dawned on me that Liam's vivaciousness, his optimism, and his contagious cheer weren't an intrusion; they were antidotes. Good medicine. A clear reminder that life has its joyous moments, too.

And, thanks to Liam's example, I learned a valuable lesson. I learned that humor heals. Hook, line, and sinker.

Carol McAdoo Rehme

Saving the Best Till Last

Miserable comforters are ye all.

Job 16:2

The clinic I worked at in a small rural town had a childhood immunization program. We often had only five clients on any given clinic day, except, that is, when it was time for school vaccinations. Then we could easily have twenty to thirty clients during our three-hour clinic.

One busy summer day a young lady, who would be entering seventh grade, came into our immunization clinic. As soon as she entered I knew this was going to take a while, as she immediately began to cry. I quietly closed the door and instructed her and her father to sit at the screener's table. I reviewed her records and explained her need for tetanus, MMR, and a series of three hepatitis B vaccines. She cried even harder and tried to leave, but her dad talked her into sitting back down and continuing with the process.

I tried to comfort her, but to no avail. I began teaching about each vaccine and she interrupted. "Do I really need to take all *three* of those shots?"

I assured her she did, and she bawled harder. I proceeded with my injection routine, explaining everything as I did. When I attempted to give the tetanus booster, she jerked away and covered the injection site with her free hand. After much coaxing, she moved her hand away, received the injection, and melted into tears again.

This scene was repeated as I finally gave the hepatitis B vaccine and, thirty minutes later, the MMR. She clung to me afterward and finally ceased crying—until I reminded her to come back the next month for her second hepatitis B. Her dad assured me they'd return. I had my doubts.

The next month, they were indeed back. I had hoped she realized this was really no big deal, but she erupted into tears as soon as she entered my room again. We repeated her routine of protest, but I finally talked her into taking her second hepatitis B—this time in only ten minutes!

I was surprised to see her back five months later, but not surprised to see the deluge of tears. I tried to cheer her up by telling her, "This is the last hepatitis B vaccination I will ever give you. I promise! But you have to have this one because this is the one that makes the vaccine work."

She looked at me with a shocked expression. "Well, why didn't you give me this one *first*?"

Delores Treffer

"You're giving me a flu shot? Shouldn't you be giving me an anti-flu shot?"

Gang-Style

Men judge generally more by the eye than by the hand, for everyone can see and few can feel. Everyone sees what you appear to be, few really know what you are.

Niccolo Machiavelli

It was six o'clock Monday morning. My twelve-hour shift in the emergency room of a county hospital was about to come to a close, and I moved through the sterile rooms, silently grateful the weekend was over. These nights are the busiest of my workweek, when we see more accidents, more drunks, more stab and gunshot wounds. But, I thought, in one hour I can go home and climb into the security and comfort of my bed . . . an inviting thought.

Then, the emergency room front-door buzzer sounded. Glancing around, I realized I was alone in the ward. This was unusual, and it made me uncomfortable. I moved hesitantly toward the half-glass door that led to an outside ramp. In the pale light that dawned just over the horizon and split through the tall pine trees around the hospital, I could make out the figures of two young black men. They were dressed in grunge, their heads wrapped in do-rags. Neither of them appeared to be in distress, and I felt a chill run through me. If they were part of a gang, I surmised, they might be here to rob the narcotics cabinet. At ninety-five pounds, I would be no match for them. Still, I unlocked the door and pushed it open.

"Can I help you?" The question sounded meek, even to me.

"We've got a man out here we think is having a heart attack," one of the young men answered.

That's when I noticed an elderly white man leaning over the cab of an old pickup truck. My nursing instincts took over. I immediately called for help. The maintenance man, who happened to be close by, aided me in getting the man into a wheelchair as the two black men rattled off their story.

"The old man drove up to the service station. Said he was having chest pains and could we tell him where the nearest hospital is. That's when we said, 'We'll take ya, man.'"

I marveled that, given their appearance, the old man had given them his keys.

We got the man into an examination room, leaving the two young men behind. As we began triage, the patient began to panic. "My dog's in the truck!"

"That's okay, sir," I soothed. "We'll have someone take care of your dog."

"You don't understand," he continued. "Mutsy's over twenty years old. She can't take the heat."

At his insistence, an orderly was sent to the truck to open the windows for the dog.

"All I have is Mutsy," the old man told us. "It's just Mutsy and me, traveling around the States."

The orderly returned with a box of pill bottles he found

on the front seat. I was stunned to see that none of the bottles had labels. One was filled with aspirin, a common prescription for heart patients.

"Sir, can you tell me how much aspirin you take a day?" I asked.

Kind, watered-down eyes focused on the bottle in my hand. "Oh, that's not mine," he informed me. "That's Mutsy's."

The respiratory therapist came in. "Carla, you've gotta see this dog! He's Benji with an overbite!"

Once our patient was stabilized, the doctor on duty told him he would need to be kept for observation.

"What about Mutsy?" he asked.

"Don't worry about Mutsy," the R.T. said. "She's going home with me."

He thanked us. "By the way," he added, "do you know who those two young men are?"

In the efficiency of my work, I had forgotten about them. "No, sir. I don't."

"They sure were nice," he said.

A quick check of the emergency area proved the men were gone.

I chastised myself as I recalled my initial reaction seeing them standing on the other side of the ER door. I wish I had taken their names so we could thank them properly. But in my heart, I knew they didn't come to the aid of the man for a pat on the back. They came because, underneath their gang-style clothing, pure hearts were beating.

Carla Tretheway
as told to Eva Marie Everson

100

*Beautiful young people are accidents of nature,
but beautiful old people are works of art.*

Eleanor Roosevelt

As a clinical instructor of nursing, my favorite unit for working with students was an orthopedic unit at Williamsport Hospital. This unit had patients with total hip and knee replacements. Taking care of these people provided a challenging medical-surgical clinical experience. The patients all had intravenous fluids, dressing changes, injections, medications, physical therapy, and patient teaching needs. My students often commented that they couldn't believe how old the patients were with most being in their seventies.

One Wednesday afternoon, I got to the unit to select our patients for the next two days. One of the nurses commented that they had just admitted a 100-year-old woman for a total hip replacement. I went in to meet Sadie and asked her permission for a student to participate in her care the next two days.

Then I had to ask, "Why at 100 would you elect to have this surgery?"

Without a moment's hesitation, she answered, "I'm having trouble getting on and off of my motorcycle."

"What?" I asked, thinking she was joking. But she wasn't.

"I live alone and ride my motorcycle every day to visit my little sisters. They're ninety-nine and ninety-seven."

Kathleen D. Pagana

off the mark.com   by Mark Parisi

SUCCESSFUL HIP REPLACEMENT

offthemark.com

ATLANTIC FEATURE © 2000 MARK PARISI

Reprinted by permission of Mark Parisi and Off the Mark. ©2000 Mark Parisi.

This Is the Way We Brush Our Teeth

She had an unequalled gift . . . of squeezing big mistakes into small opportunities.

Henry James

Long, long ago, as first-year students, we were on the floor for a short time each day. Our duties were limited to refilling water pitchers, changing flower water, dusting the room, and taking vital signs.

On one of my early mornings on the ward I was asked to clean the dentures of all the patients before breakfast. Delighted with the important assignment, I went to each room with a tray, gathered the denture cups on the nightstands of the sleeping residents, and proceeded to the workroom to fulfill my duty. I diligently cleaned the teeth under clean running water with a special brush and denture cleaner, then placed them all on the counter in a neat row. As I started to put the dentures back into each cup I suddenly froze. Although I had done a superb job of cleaning them, I now saw a dilemma, which held me suddenly suspended. I didn't know to whom the dentures belonged!

Nervously, I went to the charge nurse and confessed my problem. After she wiped tears from her eyes from her laughter, she helped me sort some that she recognized, then we set about the arduous task of fitting the remaining dentures to the appropriate residents.

Room by room, we fit and refit teeth until, hours later, each resident was smiling a gleaming smile and anticipating chomping down on breakfast.

The next day when I returned to the floor, the charge nurse began laughing again as soon as she saw me.

"Mrs. Smith's son came in last night wondering who was responsible for his mother's new teeth!"

My heart stopped. Expulsion from nursing school whirled in my mind.

"He said, 'They fit for the first time in fifteen years! We cannot thank you enough!'"

Beverly Houseman

An Alien Named Maria

If you want others to be happy, practice compassion. If you want to be happy, practice compassion.

The Dalai Lama

It was indeed a dark, stormy night, much like a classic horror film, when I met Maria. Tropical storms often flooded our department with water and excess patients.

"Alien at the door! Alien at the door!" the hospital overhead paging system announced.

UFOs hadn't landed. "Alien at the door" was the code used to announce the imminent arrival of an illegal alien to our OB department. Our visitor would probably be in very active labor and unable to speak English.

I worked as a nurse-midwife in a large inner-city hospital, which served primarily the poor and indigent. Most of our patients were young, poor, and frightened . . . especially of being deported.

To remain anonymous, the illegal immigrants developed a strange policy of literally dropping off their laboring family member at the emergency room entrance of the hospital. When a woman was in labor, someone borrowed the only working car in a neighborhood, then drove around the hospital perimeter in the junker car, trying to time the patient's arrival to within minutes of the new baby's delivery. Squealing around the circular drive to drop off their precious cargo, they hoped their timing was such that they were not caught—and the baby was.

I heard the overhead page again. "Alien at the door!"

Tonight was my turn, so I quickly donned the requisite blue gloves and ran for the elevator, expecting I would be delivering the baby, or at least the placenta, within minutes.

The elevator door opened. I saw her eyes first: wide and dilated in pain and terror. These huge chocolate-colored orbs beckoned me to help. Long black hair glistened with raindrops and perspiration as she writhed on the hospital stretcher.

Clenched fists were rigid at her sides. I tried in my limited Spanish to ask her to relax her arm. Hospital policy required an IV before delivery, if possible. But she would not, or could not, relax. As I looked at her arm, I saw she clutched something in her left hand. It appeared metallic. I wondered if it were drugs or a weapon.

I stepped back to try a different approach.

"Mucho dolor?" I asked her. (Much pain?)

"Sí, sí!" she cried.

"Lo siento, Senora." (I am sorry, ma'am.) *"Agua?"* I asked her. (Water?)

"Por favor."

I handed her a small paper cup with cold water in it, but as she reached to accept it, a deep guttural sound escaped her lips.

I dropped the cup, but managed to catch a beautiful screaming baby girl. The universal journey of a life began for this new little one. I gently handed the baby to the now sobbing mother.

"*Felicidades,*" (Congratulations) I told her.

I patted the Cuban Madonna's cheek and watched the awesome miracle again, as if for the first time.

All too quickly I heard the persistent overhead page and ran to the next emergent delivery.

The next day, I visited Maria's room and learned more of her story. She had been born in Cuba, one of eleven children. Her family had saved money for almost ten years to send one of their members to Florida. When it came time to take the dangerous trip, they chose her because they wanted her unborn baby to be born in America. The handlers in Cuba charged $8,000 to ride on a makeshift raft made of Styrofoam and inner tubes. I could not imagine being pregnant and riding for three long nights on the open ocean with twenty other people on a 10x15-foot raft.

What in life is so desperate that one must escape at all costs? What hope lies within a woman who will do anything to provide a better life for her unborn child?

Instead of feeling angry or disgusted, I felt admiration for her bravery and dedication when she told me stories of persecution, confiscation, and even torture of her family members.

Sorrowfully, Maria related how badly Americans had treated her, criticizing her for laziness, or accusing her of trying to take advantage of American tax dollars. Maria was not lazy or selfish, but courageous, motivated, and self-sacrificing. Maria wanted what every mother wants: a safe and better life for her baby

As I entered the hospital the next day, Maria was being wheeled out to the same circular driveway on which she'd been thrown out of a car only forty-eight hours earlier.

"*Buena suerte,*" I said. (Good luck.)

"*Señora Doctor,*" she called out to me. I was not a doctor, but she did not understand the difference between a mid-wife and a doctor. *"Para usted,"* she said (for you).

She reached inside the baby's blanket and brought out a beautiful silver, fan-shaped brooch. I realized that it was the same metal object she had been clenching in her hand upon her arrival at the hospital.

In Spanish, Mana told me that her favorite aunt had given it to her. "I want you to have it," she went on in Spanish.

"No!" I protested. "I cannot accept this."

I could see in her eyes that it meant everything to her that I receive this gift.

She tried to explain her feelings to me. In English, it went something like this, "You were the first American to treat me with respect since I have been here. Wear it and do not forget. There are many other women like me. It is the hope of all women, not poor or rich, but all women, to sacrifice for their children. Do not despise the steps they take to move beyond their difficult circumstances. Tell them my story."

And I have.

Cheryl Herndon

Two Choices

The strongest principle of growth lies in the human choice.

George Eliot

I enjoy working on the oncology floor, although a lot of my colleagues find it depressing. Sure, it can be sad at times, but I don't look at it as seeing people waiting to die, as much as seeing people who need others to see them as still living.

For several days I'd been assigned to give Bob his breathing treatments. We'd never met before but I was instantly impressed with his wit, however old his jokes might be.

Bob was what most people would call "a character." He always had a risqué joke that made his wife groan, laugh, and punch him in the arm. Like, "Have you heard the one about the guy who says that every year for the last three years when he goes on vacation his wife gets pregnant? Yeah, so this year he's taking her with him." Ba-dum-bum.

He asked everyone who entered the room, "How are

you today?" or, "What's new with you?"—and then he
waited for their answer. He'd never met a stranger, as my
mother used to say. He was completely open about his
life, showing everyone who came in the room photos of
his kids and grandkids, and telling us about their latest
winning game, great test score, or band concert.

He was just as open about his diagnosis. Bob had six
months to live and when he informed me of this fact, he
looked me right in the eye and the smile didn't leave his
face. He shrugged and said, "I'd really like to make it
through Christmas. I sure like all the food the Missus
cooks and having all the kids around the house."

I couldn't help myself; I had to ask.

"Bob, how can you be so happy all the time? I don't
mean to insult you in any way. I love it when I come in to
work and see your name on my list of patients, but with
your diagnosis, how do you manage to stay so positive?"

He grinned his Bob grin. "Well, it's like this. Pretty simple. I figure I have the same two choices every single day,
no matter if I'm sick or well, no matter if the doctor says
I'm dying or not. I can be happy or I can be bitter, and I'm
the only one who controls that.

"I also figure that, since the doctor has told me I'm
dying, I still have two choices. I can either make them miss
me when I'm gone, or I can make sure they're relieved that
I'm finally out of their lives. I'm still the only one who controls that too. Personally, I'd like them to miss me."

"You're right," I said.

"Not only that," he said, pointing a finger at me. "It's not
just me. You have the same two choices every day, too.
You can be happy or you can be bitter. Many people think
they have no control over their lives. Sure, there are many
things that happen that we wish could pass us by, but we
can always choose whether we're going to be happy or
bitter, and if we're going to make our family and friends

glad they know us or not. It's simple."

He was right about both of those things. It is that simple and we do always have those two choices.

I choose to be happy and I miss Bob.

Glenna Anderson Muse

8

DIVINE
INTERVENTION

Man's ultimate destiny is to become one with the Divine Power which governs and sustains the creation and its creatures.

Alfred A. Montapert

Do You Hear the Bells?

Where words fail, music speaks.

Hans Christian Andersen

It was a cold December night. I was working the 3-11 shift and we only had five patients on the pediatric ward.

As I took report, I learned that Kelly was back. Kelly, a beautiful five-year-old with leukemia and sparkling blue eyes, lost her blond ringlets after her last round of chemo. But tonight the sparkle was gone as she struggled to deal with the pain of the disease.

I volunteered to care for her. She and I were good friends and had a special relationship. When her mom was at work, I often read to her or played games when the evenings grew long and lonely.

But tonight her mom was with her too, and we both knew she was failing fast.

As I entered the room, her mother was singing softly, "Away in a Manger," and rocking Kelly. Kelly looked up, smiled weakly, and leaned into her mother's chest.

I spoke softly. "How are you feeling?"

"I'm really tired . . . but I'm waiting for Christmas," she answered just as softly.

"For Christmas?"

"Yes, I want to put the bells on the tree."

Her mother explained as she rocked, "Her uncle sent a set of bells all the way from Bethlehem and Kelly is so excited to have a gift from the birthplace of Jesus."

"Well, we will have to get you feeling better so you can get home for Christmas," I replied. I left the room quietly and went to the desk.

Kelly's chart was opened with a note from the doctor. "Pain meds per protocol for comfort. No code."

I sighed as the realization hit me that Kelly would not see Christmas.

I held back the tears as her call light came on. I entered the room to check on her and she looked at me and said, "Do you hear that noise?"

Her mother shook her head no and asked for pain medicine.

I returned quickly to the med room to draw up the dose of morphine. When I returned, Kelly was sitting up with her finger on her pursed lips.

"*Shhhhh.* Do you hear the bells? It's the bells my uncle Ben sent me. Do you hear them?"

I nodded my head as I pushed the pain med. She settled back again to snuggle against her mother's chest.

"What do I do?" her mother asked.

I just shook my head, and whispered a prayer with her. As I left, Kelly was resting quietly.

When I returned later, Kelly was awake and smiled as I entered the room.

"The bells are calling me," she said. "I'm going . . . I'm going to be with Jesus's, bells." With that, she took a deep breath—and was gone.

Her mother and I were crying softly together when

suddenly, out of the dark night, the sound of tiny bells pierced the silence.

"She did hear the bells," her mother sighed, "and she's home for Christmas."

Judy Whorton

"I would have been here sooner,
if not for a wonderful caring nurse in the hospital."

A Mysterious Intervention

Those who learn to know death, rather than to
fear and fight it, become our teachers about life.

Elisabeth Kübler-Ross

Nancy had a heart for those facing death. As a hospice
nurse, she journeyed with them right up to their point of
departure and saw glimpses into the unknown that most
people never see. Nancy loved her work. "I wouldn't have
any other job," she said.

That was her sentiment before she encountered David.

A young man, David lay in his hospice bed facing the
wall. Angry and frightened, he didn't speak to the staff or
to his wife, Julia. He had undergone painful, radical neck
surgery, radiation, and chemotherapy, hoping for a chance
at life, hoping to continue his good job and happy marriage. But the cancer returned with a vengeance. Disfigured and with no hope left, he felt his feelings were
justified.

"How do we deal with this unfortunate man?" Nancy
asked. The nursing staff tried many approaches: counseling,

medications, conversations, invitations, anything to try and gain his participation in his own care and reduce his suffering. But these interventions all failed. He responded to their efforts with no eye contact, no verbal interaction, and a rigid body position that faced the wall.

Nancy had joined hospice because of the special, caring relationship opportunities it presented. Day after day, she took time with each patient. The philosophy at hospice was clear: "We are all in this together and we will help each other get through it."

But there was no possibility of such teamwork with David. The palpable gloom in his room made Nancy's former nursing duties look vastly preferable. She would have welcomed the chance to be overloaded with hospital tasks, or be undone by a complicated baby delivery, or buried in bandages in the burn unit. Even the nursing home patient who called her "nefarious" would be a welcome change from David's silent despair.

For the first time in her hospice career, Nancy felt eager and relieved to go off duty.

The next day she returned to find that David had lapsed into unconsciousness. Cold and clammy, his color was gray, pulse and respirations very slow. Thinking perhaps he had slipped into a diabeticlike coma, a blood sugar test was taken but found normal. He did not respond to the lancet sticking his finger or to Julia calling his name. The nurses were sure the end must be near.

About an hour went by and much to their surprise, he woke up. He seemed dazed but he immediately turned his body position away from the wall and toward the door. Most amazing of all, he smiled and made conversation.

"Where were you this past hour?" Julia asked. "You seemed so far away. What happened?"

Very calmly, he replied, "I have been somewhere else." Then with a peaceful expression, he refused to say any more about it. He spent the rest of the day quietly talking with his wife and interacting with the hospice staff.

That evening, Nancy answered his light and assisted him to the bathroom. "I appreciate your help," he said. "Thank you for everything."

"You are most welcome. How is your pain tonight?" she asked.

"I don't have pain anymore," he responded, then he talked calmly and openly about the reality of his condition.

He walked comfortably beside Nancy back to his bed. She felt he would have a good night's sleep.

A little later, the nurse at his bedside called Nancy in. "He's dead."

Surprised, Nancy looked at him. He did not appear dead. Further investigation confirmed, however, that he was without vital signs. The most unusual thing she noticed was the beautiful smile on his calm, peaceful face. While observing him, Nancy felt peace and quietness come over her.

She reflected that David's death was not at all like that of the "nefarious" man who had died like he lived, with a curse on his lips and a contorted expression on his face. David's death was more like the majority of her patients who, in their last moments, saw beautiful gardens, long-dead relatives, white light, angel-like beings, a long passageway with someone at the end. Others heard conversations, music, or someone inviting them to "Come." Others talked about going home or to work, or having to do something, or get something straight.

Nancy and Julia agreed that David in his suffering had experienced a mysterious intervention. He had been taken somewhere and seen something wonderful.

"And best of all," added Nancy, "he came back to show us that he was all right and no longer afraid."

Through her tears, Julia took Nancy's hand and squeezed it. "Thank you."

Nancy's heart spilled over.

What she received from patients nearing death, she gave to others facing life.

Margaret Lang with Nancy Madson

Laura's Story

Every believer is God's miracle.

Gamaliel Bailey

I stood in the middle of the living room waiting to meet
Laura for the first time. My eyes rested on a framed photo
atop the television set. In it lived a beguiling young
woman with soft curly auburn hair, a winsome smile, and
large azure eyes peeking beneath dark arched brows. I
wondered at the joyous spirit reflected in Laura's face but
soon learned that the spark radiating from her eyes was
not a trick of the camera.

Though congenital hydrocephalus, cerebral palsy,
numerous surgeries, and rigorous medical regimens had
taken a physical toll, those trials never dampened Laura's
spirit. In spite of her weakened condition, Laura still pro-
jected the smiling innocence and radiant energy reflected
in the photo.

This twenty-year-old who remained an ingratiating
woman-child captivated me, her hospice nurse. Laura had
never met a stranger, never learned about evil or enemies.

I witnessed her grab and kiss the hand of friends—new or old—and pour forth the blessing of her smiling, unconditional love. Her spontaneous questions and dauntless curiosity endeared many hearts, including mine.

One day during my routine visit, Laura said, "I'm going to be a secretary someday," and proceeded to tell me her dreams for the future. She had also shared this dream with her doctor, and soon he and his staff helped Laura "be a secretary." Because her weakened condition prevented her from visiting the doctor's office, the doctor's office came to Laura. Photos taped to the wall around her bed documented her in her bedroom, surrounded by telephone and typewriter, smiling valiantly and proficiently, carrying out her secretarial duties, realizing her dream.

Caring for Laura was a family affair. She was especially close to her beloved grandfather, who devoted many hours of loving attention to accommodating Laura's disabilities. He built a special cart in which she rode as he pulled her around the neighborhood, meeting and greeting neighbors, stopping for occasional friendly chats.

One day during a reflective moment at the kitchen table, Laura's mom, Roseanna, shared that Laura had been one of triplets born prematurely. Laura's two sisters, Libby and Chrissy, died shortly after birth, a fact that had never been discussed with Laura.

Soon after hearing this story, I was summoned to Laura's home. Her condition had worsened. Roseanna met me at the door and, in spite of her fatigue and grief, I sensed an air of expectancy. After ensuring that Laura was comfortable, Roseanna invited me once again to rest a moment at the kitchen table, sharing yet another story.

Two nights before, Laura had been restless and Roseanna crawled into bed with her, lying "spoon fashion" to comfort her daughter. In the morning Laura awakened and whispered to her mom, "I'm tired and I'm ready."

Roseanna lay still beside Laura, her quiet presence encouraging her to reveal more. "Besides," Laura added softly, "my sisters are waiting for me. I saw them standing in the doorway to my room."

Stunned by Laura's revelation, but soothed by her acceptance and readiness for death, Roseanna comforted Laura, giving her permission to go, reassuring her that those left behind would be fine. More peaceful now, Laura returned to sleep.

Roseanna then lifted herself gently from the bed and wandered to the front door of the house. Still contemplating Laura's words, she struggled to understand how Laura could know about her sisters, wondering what or who Laura had really seen. As she opened the front door, sunshine and crisp morning air greeted her, momentarily easing her grief. Only a large, shady ash tree stood at attention in the center of a bare green lawn. Roseanna had so little time to care for a yard and always promised herself that one day she would make time to plant some flowers. As her eyes scanned the yard, a colorful spot under Laura's bedroom window captured her attention. Closer inspection revealed three pink rain lilies, lazily intertwined. These flowers had not been there the day before. In fact, she had never seen them before in the many years they'd lived there.

And now, here I sat the next day, rising from the kitchen chair as Roseanna led me outside to the front lawn. Pointing to a spot under Laura's bedroom window, I saw the once colorful lilies, now muted, their gray stems loosely blended into the soil that once sustained them.

As I left Laura's home on the day she died, I lingered on the front lawn. The spot below her window was barren now with no visible sign of the earlier visitors.

Yet I knew their legacy remained.

Patricia J. Gardner

The Infant

It is difficult to make a man miserable while he feels worthy of himself and claims kindred to the great God who made him.

Abraham Lincoln

As my eight-year-old daughter and seven-year-old son climbed into our car, I drew in the crisp December air and smiled. I had a few days off from the hectic nursing pace of a cardiac step-down unit. My mind raced with things to do—holiday cookies to bake, stockings to fill. We had enjoyed a visit with relatives in a neighboring town. The day was topped off with a bag of hand-me-downs. As a single mother, I was pleased to receive the gently used clothing for the children.

We drove home on the country road, talking and laughing as we approached the intersection near an old church. The wind increased, and I slowed the car as I anticipated slippery conditions from blowing snow. Ahead, I could see an eerie haze. As we got closer, I realized it was radiator steam from cars involved in a collision.

Parking next to the church, I grabbed the first-aid kit and ordered my wide-eyed children to remain in the car. I hurried toward the accident, careful not to slip on the packed snow. I was the first responder. No one was in the first car. The scene at the other car was surreal. A man sat on the ground. A dazed woman sat behind the steering wheel. Two small children looked up at me from under the dashboard. My nursing experience, infused with adrenalin, kicked into high gear.

A driver from a delivery service appeared at my side. "I was a paramedic once," he shouted.

"Assess any passengers in the backseat while I assess the front."

A group of gawkers was forming. I looked at a nearby burly guy, "Sit by the man on the ground and hold his hand."

He snorted. "I'm not holding his hand."

"I am in charge of the crash you have stopped to look at," I retorted. "Sit down and hold his hand or drive away."

He knelt next to the man and spoke softly as he took his hand.

Two LPNs stopped. I put them in charge of the children under the dashboard. Someone opened the church, and they took the children inside. I sent another bystander to my car for the bag of clothing to be used as bandages for the youngsters.

As I leaned toward the woman behind the steering wheel, the former paramedic tapped my shoulder.

"How are you with babies?" he asked.

"A baby?" I hadn't heard crying! The paramedic and I switched places. I carefully pulled the child carrier out of the backseat and gazed into the sweet face of a still infant swaddled in a gray blanket. Since I didn't know the extent of trauma, I left the baby in the car seat and quickly walked to the open door of the delivery van. With the carrier seat as my backboard and the van floor as my flat surface, I started CPR. Two fingers across the tiny chest, puffs of air into the lungs. As I puffed, I could smell the sweet baby scent. With each puff, I begged God. With each compression, I whispered, "Come on, baby, cry! Please don't die. I'm giving you all I've got. Lord, help us."

An air ambulance landed. As the crew scrambled to assess the injured, one member looked over my shoulder. "Keep doing CPR," he said. "You're doing great. We'll get set up and take over."

Within minutes, he carried the baby aboard the helicopter. Other members of the family were transported via air and ground to a local trauma center.

I took a deep breath and walked to my car as wreckers hoisted twisted metal onto flatbeds.

"What happened, Mommy?" my children pleaded. We prayed for the family, with the infant's face and sweet scent firmly planted in my senses. I pondered my recent CPR instructor training class when I had drawn the card with the words *Infant CPR*. To earn instructor status, I studied the technique well. I also thought of the bag of clothing used as bandages. It was all part of God's plan.

After we got home, I went outside to breathe crisp air, to cry, and to pray. As I opened my eyes, I saw through tears a small grayish blue creature watching me. It meowed. A kitten out in the cold! I called to it, but it didn't move.

"You must be hungry," I said. "Wait here."

I hurried back with an opened can of tuna fish, but the kitten was gone. I looked for paw prints in the snow, ready to follow the tracks. But nothing. How could there be a kitten and snow, but no paw prints?

It hit me. The kitten was the same gray as the blanket and clothing the sweet baby had worn. In that moment, I knew: the baby was in the arms of God. The kitten had come to tell me, "You tried really hard. You did all you could."

I wiped away more tears and went inside to call the hospital where the family had been transported. When I was connected with the pediatric ICU, I explained my interest in the baby. The nurse drew in a breath, clearly struggling whether to reveal information to me.

Finally, she said, "The baby is brain-dead. They're transporting his mother over to discontinue life support. They are donating his organs. You gave him every chance by doing CPR. Now another child will be saved because of your efforts to save this one."

Her voice trailed off as we both cried.

I learned a new lesson that day. As nurses our degrees and certifications have trained us well. However, even with all those initials behind our names, we must remember we are lacking three: G-O-D.

We do our part, but the outcome is up to Him.

Thea Picklesimer
as told to Sandra P. Aldrich

I See Glory

There are only two kinds of people in the end: those who say to God, "Thy will be done," and those to whom God says, in the end, "Thy will be done."

C. S. Lewis

Ms. Sally was a frail woman with totally white coarse hair. Her skin was so ebony it appeared a deep hue of blue. Her tiny frame was curled in the fetal position. She didn't respond to painful stimuli or loving gestures. It was difficult to position her body using pillows with all her muscles contractured. It didn't keep me from trying to make her comfortable. She looked like someone's grandma lying there, but no one was at her bedside. I checked her chart and learned she was a patient from the local nursing home. She had one son who lived in Arizona. She was alone.

I worked the midnight shift, 11:00 PM to 7:00 AM. I was a new nurse and very unsure of myself, but that was a good thing as far as the patients were concerned. I made extra

rounds every night to make sure my patients were comfortable, IVs were running on time, and to catch any
potential problems early.

If the night was quiet, I gave a couple of baths in the
early mornings to the patients who were already awake,
or the ones whose condition was such that a warm bath
would only make them feel better. Ms. Sally, the little
granny, was one patient that I paid the extra attention to.
Her living ninety-three years only to be dying alone
tugged at my heartstrings. I bathed her with warm soapy
water and tried to be careful and keep her modesty as to
maintain her dignity in her last days. I turned her and
lotioned her and sang old hymns quietly the entire time.
Both of my grannies loved hymns and I assumed all elderly people did. She quickly became my favorite patient.

In the ten days she was in the hospital, she never spoke
a word. She never acknowledged my presence. She never
even moaned when I faithfully turned her every two
hours. One night I was humming "Amazing Grace" and
actually thought I saw the corners of her mouth turn up.
Maybe a smile? No, that couldn't be possible. The doctors had
assured me she was truly comatose.

One day when I came on my shift I immediately went
to Ms. Sally's room. She had been in my dreams during
my sleep that day. I opened the door and saw her covered
with perspiration. Her eyes were open and glassy. As I put
my stethoscope to her back, it sounded as if her lungs
were full of water. I immediately called the doctor and
after much encouragement from me, he ordered IV antibiotics. I made my other rounds and everyone else was status quo. I knew, if possible, I'd spend the biggest part of
my shift in her room. I did not want this little woman to
die alone. I called her son in Arizona and discussed her
condition. He knew she was in the hospital, but had no
idea she was dying. The man was also elderly, in very poor

health, and unable to travel. I couldn't help myself, and before we hung up I asked him, "Does your mother love the Lord?"

"She is the closest thing to a saint I've ever known."

My instincts were right.

When Ms. Sally's pulse began to get very irregular, I called the doctor again. By this time it was 3:30 AM and he wasn't happy with me. "The woman is old and dying, Sue!"

Reluctantly, he ordered the EKG I'd requested.

The tech was in the room with me when Ms. Sally's respirations grew very shallow and nearly absent. She still had the EKG tabs attached to her when all of a sudden, she slowly straightened herself and sat up in the bed! She stretched her skinny withered arms toward the heavens. Her eyes were no longer glassy but she didn't appear to see anything around her in the room either.

She spoke in a crackly voice just above a whisper, "I see Glory . . . it's so beau-ti-ful!" She fell back on the pillow and the EKG machine blasted a siren. Her heart had stopped beating. She was in the glory of heaven where all faithful saints spend eternity.

Sue Henley

Our Daily Bread

Duty is ours, results are God's.

John Quincy Adams

Working as the camp nurse for multihandicapped children brings an array of joys—and frustrations. Many of the children can't talk or communicate in any way. Days with these kids are "conversations" of crude hand gestures on the kids' parts, and educated guesses for the adults, as campers use sign language to indicate they need to go to the bathroom, want something to eat, or are feeling pain.

Stan, a senior counselor, and I were in the infirmary one night after most of our happy campers were fast asleep. In walked two discouraged junior counselors with Tony, an autistic sixteen-year-old, who was obviously hurting and signing that he was in pain.

"Please take a look at him," one counselor begged. "Something's really bothering him. He keeps signing 'pain' but we can't find anything wrong."

"It's okay, Tony," I comforted, while Stan and I got him

onto a cot. "I'll fix you up." But I failed. I did the usual exam: no fever, red throat, or excessive bug bites. Tony, with a tortured expression and soft moans, signed over and over, counting on me to relieve his hurt.

After one more unsuccessful attempt to diagnose, I ruled out anything serious. I stroked Tony's head. "I'm sorry, fella, I just don't see the culprit. I wish you could tell me more." But I knew from within his private world that was impossible.

Stan took one arm and I took the other to support Tony's unsteady gait, as we stepped out into a glorious night to take him back to his cabin.

Struggling to deal with Tony's upset and my own feelings of ineptness, I suggested the only thing I could think of.

"I know, guys, let's pray while we walk."

Stan started off in a booming voice, "Our Father . . . "

Immediately, Tony stopped. He placed his fingers, palm to palm, like praying hands, and his indistinguishable sounds became a singsong pattern resembling, "Who art in heaven . . . "

"Stan, he knows the Lord's Prayer. He knows! That's right, Tony, we'll pray the Lord's Prayer."

There under the brilliance of His stars, Stan and I repeated the Lord's Prayer. Tony's soft moans changed to a rhythmic monotone, the only way he could pray along.

When we said, "Give us this day our daily bread," I silently added, *Please Lord, you know what we need.* And as we arrived at "Amen," Tony unfolded his hands and reached down to his right heel.

By the glow of the moon, I removed Tony's brand-new tennis shoe to reveal a huge, raw blister. We took him back to the infirmary, where I applied soothing cream and a big fluffy bandage to ease his discomfort.

I stood in the doorway, watching a now serene Tony

helped back to his cabin by Stan and another counselor. And I marveled that what four adults could not figure out, God had reached past the fog of a little boy's mind and made crystal clear.

Sharon Weinland Georges
as told to Judith Weinland Justice

Another Wavelength

God made Truth with many doors to welcome every believer who knocks on them.

Kahlil Gibran

When I was a young nurse, we had a patient in our hospital who, although gravely ill, did not want to talk about this subject, nor did he want to pray. Although the doctors warned him that it was time to give these matters serious thought, he seemed not to hear it. "Oh, I'll make peace with the Lord when the time comes," he said to me with a wink.   Despite this, he was a lovable, cooperative, cheerful man with a great enthusiasm for life and a generous interest in others. The one cherished object he had managed to bring with him to the hospital was a shortwave radio, which he kept on a nightstand next to his bed.

As I cared for other patients, I passed his room, which was right next to the nurses' station. Each time I passed, I said a little prayer. And each time I passed, he called out loudly, "Anne, come and listen! I think I've tuned in

Rhodesia"—or some other faraway country that held for him some particular fascination.

Too busy to stop at his request one afternoon, I laughed in response to his usual invitation to "Come listen!" and told him I couldn't stop right then. "But be sure to tell me," I joked, "if you tune in heaven!"

A few days later, he had a major stroke. Already severely ill, this added to his rapidly weakening condition. He was no longer able to speak, except for an occasional word or two, and this with great difficulty.

One night I went into his room with his medications and his enteral feeding, and I lingered longer than usual, trying to find some way of making him more comfortable. For once, the shortwave radio remained silent. He struggled to breathe.

While I was adjusting the bed linens, he tugged on my sleeve, indicating that he wanted to tell me something. I bent close to his ear. He smiled weakly with a twinkle in his eye. With great difficulty, he managed to form these words with his last breaths:

"I did it, Anne . . . I . . . finally . . . tuned in . . . heaven!"

Anne Wilson

I'm Going to Die!

And we know that all things work together for good to them that love God.

Romans 8:28

I'm going to die!
The words pierced my soul. Everything around me was spinning. I put down the telephone and replayed the conversation in my mind.

"Kathy, your HIV test . . . it's come back positive!" my doctor had blurted out.

In shock, I stared out the window. My worst nightmare had come true.

Back in June 1986, I was a nurse working in the ER when an accident-related trauma patient was wheeled in. We cracked open his chest to perform internal CPR. My bare hands were wrist-deep inside him. Despite our best efforts, he died minutes later.

Later that night, we found out he had AIDS. My own heart skipped a beat as I looked down at my hands and remembered a minor cut on my right index finger. As you know, back in the mid-1980s, we didn't wear gloves to protect us.

The doctors decided to run additional tests to confirm the positive results. My nightmare continued. Weeks later, eight confirmatory tests also came back positive. The doctors notified the Centers for Disease Control (CDC), who were also concerned.

You see, I was the first healthcare worker in America to ever test HIV-positive from an on-the-job exposure.

Back then, AIDS was a guaranteed death sentence. Most AIDS victims did not survive more than a year. Speculation was rampant, but no one really knew all the ways it could be spread.

No, this can't happen to me, I thought angrily. *I can't handle it! What am I going to do? I am a nurse just trying to help someone!* It was more than I could bear.

Reluctantly, that night I sat down and tearfully told my family.

Then, after mentally laboring for days, I forced myself to tell my boss. She was sympathetic, but said, "Kathy, if this gets out, this hospital will shut down. I'm sorry, but you can't work here anymore."

That weekend, I shared the shocking news with my church. To my amazement, some members turned away from me. I overheard one say, "You know AIDS is God's punishment." Another member whispered, "Don't touch her, you'll take it home to your kids!"

I stopped eating. I stopped sleeping.

One night in a graduate school class, as I wrestled with my own demons, my professor showed a film, *Living with AIDS.* Sitting in the classroom, in disbelief, I watched young people at the prime of their lives wasting away in hospitals. My classmates talked in hushed tones about the horror of the disease. If they only knew who was sitting beside them . . .

That night I determined one thing: I was not going to die the slow, agonizing death of an AIDS victim. I was not going to waste away. I could not. I would not. I would choose how I would die.

After class, I got in my car. I started driving, my mind racing. It raced for hours around a track called "regrets." Regrets about not spending more time with my family and friends. I was always too busy, too stressed. Regrets about not taking the time to find out who Kathy Dempsey really was.

Finally, I found myself in the parking lot of Chattanooga's most famous hotel. I was about to add to its legend. All alone, I sat in my car that dark, drizzling night with a bottle of sleeping pills in my hand. Slowly I counted them.

One . . . two . . . three . . . four . . . five . . . six . . . seven . . . eight . . . nine . . . ten . . . No ten, that isn't enough. I've seen too many people survive on ten. I better take them all.

Three knocks on my car window jolted me back into reality. Robin, one of my friends, appeared from out of nowhere. "Kathy, are you okay?"

With tears streaming down my face, I shook my head, "No. I'm scared. I'm lonely. I'm dying!"

Robin climbed into the car beside me. "Hold on to hope," she soothed.

"Why should I go on? There is no hope!" I responded in despair.

For hours we sat and talked and cried. For every foreboding fear I stated, Robin had a beam of hope. Somehow this angel got me through the night.

My life and this story did not end there.

Three months after my initial test, I received another phone call from my doctor.

"Kathy, I am not sure how to tell you this. It's almost unbelievable . . . but your tests, all eight of your tests . . .

have come back negative. The CDC says you are not HIV-positive!"

There was the longest silence over the phone. I took a deep breath and hung up. I'm going to live! *I'm going to live!* No words had ever felt so joyous! I felt like a thousand-pound weight had been lifted from my chest.

Some people call it a medical error; I call it a miracle. A gift. It was my wake-up call. I thought my life was over, and now I had it back. Like a VCR tape, I got to push "rewind." All the regrets I had back in the car, I could amend. I fell to my knees, and promised myself from that day forward, "I will not live my life the same way again."

In a strange and crooked way, the events of a dying man's life changed mine forever.

Kathy B. Dempsey

[EDITORS' NOTE: *Twenty years later, Kathy volunteered in Africa helping orphans who lost parents to AIDS. She established the Keep Shedding Educational Foundation to support her efforts. Visit www.keepshedding.com/foundation.htm.*]

His Heart

*There are times when God asks nothing of his
children except silence, patience, and tears.*

C. S. Robinson

As I rode the elevator to my evening shift on the seventh floor of the cardiac step-down unit, I wondered, *Did
anyone get a heart today?*

I looked over my assignments and noticed a new name.
Ah, a fresh audience for my elephant jokes. Robert, as I
will call him, had been diagnosed with cardiomyopathy
and was awaiting a heart transplant. I read his chart, then
put on my best smile as I stepped into his room to introduce myself. His wife was at his bedside, but stood to kiss
him good-bye as I entered. She needed to make the long
drive home, she said, to care for their two boys, ages nine
and ten.

Robert was a quiet man in his late thirties and a long
way from home. Every day his family stayed in touch by
telephone and letters, but they could not visit often. Tall
and thin, Robert walked the halls for exercise. Wearing our

blue issued pj's and blue-striped robe with matching slippers, he always looked the same. Even in the hospital
attire, he was neat and usually smiling.

Tethered to our floor by his portable telemetry unit,
Robert was a hostage. Sometimes he roamed out of range,
and the central monitor alarm alerted me of his "escape." I
always knew where I would find him . . . by the windows
overlooking the helicopter landing pad.

After yet another alarm, I walked to Robert's window
seat. He greeted me with "Hi, Warden! I know I'm out of
range."

I smiled and stepped closer. "How you doing today,
Robert?"

He nodded toward the landing pad. "Thea, I watch the
copters come and go. I keep wondering if my heart is out
there. I have asked God to help me not to be selfish in
wanting this heart. I know for me to live someone must
die. And loved ones are faced with making a choice; a
choice to donate the organs."

I nodded and gently led him back within range.

Robert stayed on our unit for more than thirty days. I
became his link to the outside world, giving him daily
weather reports, commenting on current events, telling
countless elephant jokes—anything to keep him laughing
and comfortable. After a month of in-hospital days, some
patients may show their cabin fever by being irritable. Not
Robert. I knew he was having a bad day only when his
door was closed. And he didn't close his door often.

One evening as I checked his vital signs, he sighed. "I'm
having a really tough day. I miss my family. It's been so
long since I've seen my boys. I didn't even go to the window today."

Later that evening, I learned there was a confirmed
donor and match for Robert. Suddenly, the unit flew into
a frenzied heart-prep mode. I was pleased to be on duty

for this moment, especially since I was scheduled for vacation the following week. *Thank you, Lord, for such good timing. Bless the family whose loved one has died. Thank you for the gift of life they gave to another.*

Robert's wife and sons arrived and the air was electric as joyful tears flowed. After the final preps, I placed the blue surgical cap on Robert's head. "Make certain you come and see me when you get the color back in your cheeks."

He smiled. "Thea, I won't leave this place till I come up and see you."

With that, the OR team wheeled Robert to the surgical suite to begin the cardiac transplantation. From there, he would spend several days in ICU.

I returned from my vacation well rested and was working with a nurse we called "Mother Teresa." In addition to sharing my belief in God, she was a person to count on. As we prepared the 6:00 PM meds, we made small talk.

I looked down the hall. There was Robert, walking toward me in his usual blue pj's, blue-striped robe, and matching slippers, with his hands in his pockets and a beautiful smile on his face. I waved to him excitedly and said to Theresa, "There's Robert. He looks great!"

Then I felt her firm but gentle hand on mine. I turned to look into Mother Teresa's soft blue eyes. I stared at her for a moment, then said, "No one's there. Right, Mother?"

As she squeezed my hand, I searched her face for any hint she might think I was losing my mind. Instead she said, "I believe you saw Robert. But no one is there."

She hugged me, but I quickly pulled away. "Oh, Teresa, I need to go to ICU. Robert said he would not leave until he came to say good-bye. He always kept his word."

I hurried to the fourth-floor ICU. "Which room is Robert in?" The desk clerk gave the number but then added, "He's in cardiac arrest."

My spirits sank. I stepped to Robert's doorway and watched the heroic efforts of the doctors and nurses to bring him back. I sent up frantic prayers for his recovery and left while the code was still in progress.

Back on my floor, I told Teresa that Robert was in cardiac arrest. We prayed together for him, then got word that he died.

I smiled as I wiped away tears. Robert had kept the promise he made to me. He came to see me before he left this place.

Thea Picklesimer
as told to Sandra P. Aldrich

9

HOPE

Until the day when God shall deign to reveal the future to man, all human wisdom is summed up in these two words—"Wait and hope."

Alexandre Dumas

The Reason

While there's life, there's hope.

Cicero

Little Emily should not have been admitted to our intensive care unit. *Why didn't the EMTs take her to the nearby children's hospital?* I lamented. At eighteen months, she was too old for our hospital's newborn intensive care, and severe brain damage made her too unstable to transport. So here she was in adult ICU, stuck between an elderly woman with double pneumonia and a man with a fresh cardiac bypass.

Emily's last prehospital day had dawned cold and clear. After being cooped inside with the recent snow, her mother decided to take her for an outing. She bundled up her little daughter, put her in the stroller, and set out on a walk along their country lane. The bright sun was beginning to warm the air, and Emily delighted in pointing at the snow melting on the side of the road.

It was the snow that was her undoing. As a car came over the next hill, the sun reflected off the white surface and temporarily blinded the driver. He didn't see Emily or her mom. His car struck the stroller and sent the baby flying thirty feet where she landed on her head. Her mother was uninjured.

When doctors first examined Emily, her pupils were dilated and fixed. They immediately took her to surgery, but there was little they could do. "Her entire right hemisphere is oatmeal," one neurosurgeon said. "She'll never walk or talk again. I doubt she'll even make it out of the hospital."

I first saw Emily a week after the accident. *Well, at least she's still with us,* I thought as I looked at my beautiful little patient. Her wispy blond hair was replaced by a puffy, red suture line on the right side of her head. *The hair might grow back one day,* I thought, *but nothing will replace the damaged brain cells inside.* I did my best to take care of Emily using the pediatric equipment we improvised, but fretted over the hopelessness of her situation.

The immensity of the tragedy became even more clear whenever I saw Emily's mother. Grief and guilt aged that young woman more than forty years could have. She would stand at her baby's bedside and pat her little hand, crying bitter tears. It was more than I could bear to watch. *Why couldn't they have taken her to the pediatric hospital?* I thought.

Gradually, however, we weaned Emily off the ventilator. Finally, her pulmonary doctor ordered the evening nurse to remove her endotracheal tube. Emily breathed on her own, and her mother rejoiced. Later, on the night shift, I heard mewing sounds from Emily's room. I thought at first she was trying to cry but soon realized she was "crowing," a sound caused by strictures in her trachea. Back went the ET tube. I wrapped my arms around Emily's mother as she cried over this latest injustice.

Two days later, the tube came out for good, but there

was still no response, no indication that Emily would ever know anyone or anything. *A "vegetable," that's what people will call her,* I thought. *Her mother will be taking care of her until she dies. So sad.*

Eventually the doctors deemed Emily stable enough to move to the pediatric floor. At least I would not have to watch as her mother tried in vain to get her to say "Mama" or "wata," two words she could say before her accident.

Five weeks passed, and I forced myself not to think about Emily. After all, I knew what the outcome of her situation would be.

One night, a pediatric nurse visited the ICU and announced, "Emily's going home tomorrow."

Good, I thought, *at least her mother can take her home and care for her forever.*

"Not only that, but she's reaching for her mother, calling her 'Mama,' and asking for 'wata'!"

The next day, as they prepared to leave, Emily walked across the room into her mother's arms.

It was then I knew the reason Emily had come to our adult intensive care unit.

She came to show me that we must never give up, no matter how grave the situation seems, or how many experts tell us the outcome is futile.

She came to teach me hope.

Tracy Crump

An Easter Lesson

*Sorrows are our best educators. A man can see
further through a tear than a telescope.*

Lord Byron

Only a year had passed since my father died and I was
still very much mourning him. It was Easter weekend and
Mass was being offered in his honor. I needed to be there
with my family. Unfortunately, due to a staffing shortage,
my shift in the intensive care nursery was extended to
twelve hours and I'd miss this crucial time of commemo-
ration. To make matters worse I was assigned the care of a
baby who had been born with no kidneys and a host of
associated problems, and would surely not live more than
a couple of days. I didn't need to deal with the inevitable
emotions that threatened to overwhelm my already fragile heart.

"That's it! I'll be home soon, because I'm *quitting!*" I
fumed as my husband patiently endured my fit.

When I finished ranting, he sternly informed me, "You
will *not* quit your job. Any other time, and for any other

reason I would back you up 100 percent—but not today. You need to be there for that family and minister to them as you would have wanted somebody to minister to you last year, if you had known that your father was only going to live a couple more days."

Ugh, I thought wryly, *I hate when he's right.*

During my breakdown in the nurses' lounge, the attending physician had noticed the obvious rift and segregation among family members in the waiting area. He ordered a meeting of the staff and family—including grandparents, uncles, and aunts—to be held in the mother's room.

When the tight gathering convened, the doctor, with obvious difficulty, began, "I have sad news to share but please listen to what I have to say and then I will take questions."

He turned to the teenage couple, "You two are so young to be in this situation. Your parents may not understand, but they were trying to protect and guide you, and now, you're faced with any parent's worst nightmare. Your baby will probably not survive this weekend."

There was a uniform gasp, followed by rapt silence.

He went on to explain more in depth the infant's condition. The family begged that something be done. No, the doctor assured, it was medically impossible.

Then he continued, now facing the relatives. "Let me set some ground rules right now. I don't want anyone to criticize, condemn, or judge these young parents. What they need right now is your unconditional love and support. No fighting, no gossiping, no blaming. Just accept this child and your kids. This is hard enough as it is."

After his speech the room was still, save for the tears falling down broken faces. The doctor hugged the parents and left the room.

I followed him out and tapped him on the shoulder. "I'm

so proud of how you handled that. You look like you could use a hug too."

He gratefully accepted as his eyes welled up, and through quivering lips managed, "Thanks . . . thank you."

I returned to the ICN with a renewed purpose. Together with the family we took locks of the baby's hair, made footprints, took pictures, and created all the precious memories that families of newborns cherish. It was a special time for all, but I suspect, mainly for me. I didn't want to be there that day, but that is precisely where God wanted me.

I discovered a few things that Easter. That sometimes in the midst of great sorrow, tragedy even, people are knit together in a dramatic way. And one doctor, unable to mend that tiny body, was able to miraculously repair a devastating scenario.

Best of all, I found out that ministering hope to others going through a bad time can be the best medicine for a hurting heart.

Sylvia Martinez
as told to Barbara Cueto

A Peaceful Day

Peace I leave with you, my peace I give you.

John 14:27

It was dark outside when I climbed into my car with a cup of coffee in one hand and my bag in the other. My clogs were covered with mud from sloshing in the swamp that used to be my lawn. Before I could slam the car's door shut, a mosquito flew in and buzzed at my face.

As I backed out of the driveway, my view of the street was obstructed by silhouettes of tree trunks stacked on the curb. Two weeks ago the hurricane had hit and the neighborhood still looked like a war zone. The windshield wiper screeched as it wiped the muggy mist off the glass. I turned the radio on. The Christian music usually relaxed me.

Not today.

I turned the radio off.

Keeping my eye on the road, I brought the cup of coffee to my lips just as the mosquito attacked my eyelid. I slammed the coffee cup in the holder, suppressing a painful scream from my burned lips. The mosquito buzzed past my face again, and with my peripheral vision I saw it land on the window. My wedding band hit the glass so hard, my finger stung. I couldn't resist looking at the carcass flattened on the glass. Smiling, I looked back up to see a red traffic light. In a panic, I hit the brakes. My bag flipped, spilling all of its contents on the floor.

My self-control now gone, I choked the steering wheel. I took a deep breath. *God, please give me peace today.* I needed it to face a twelve-hour shift in the operating room where I worked as a surgical nurse. "Please, God, give me peace," I repeated.

I turned the radio back on. The song's lyric said, "He will hold you in His arms."

"I hope so," I muttered.

Pulling into the last parking space in the garage, I sipped the cold coffee and gathered the spilled contents back into my bag. Flipping the visor mirror, I scratched the welt above my eye and flicked the mosquito off the window. As I reached the garage elevators, the metal doors shut in my face just before I could step in.

My footsteps echoed in the stairwell as I ran down the stairs. I pushed open the garage door to a sunny day as other stragglers in scrubs raced toward the time clock. The massive hospital building appeared farther away than usual.

Once inside, my destination was still a long way off. I wove in and out between people in the hallways. As I sprinted around a corner, a familiar picture on the wall caught my eye. I rushed past it every day and never took notice of its message. Today, I slowed down enough to read the caption under a painting of Jesus: "Come to me all you who are weary and burdened and I will give you rest."

"I hope so," I muttered, "and I'm still waiting for peace."

In the OR, the assignment board had every grid filled with rooms, procedures, and names of surgeons, nurses, techs, and anesthesia personnel. I searched for my name. I was assigned to pediatric surgery, which was scheduled to start at 8:30 instead of the usual 7:30.

The charge nurse approached me, took one look at my face, put his arms over my shoulders, and said, "Get your room ready and then get yourself a coffee break."

The verse came back to me, " . . . and I will give you rest."

In OR 21, I checked the surgical supplies, drugs, and equipment while the anesthesiologist checked the anesthesia machine and added drops of bubble-gum scent to the plastic breathing mask. After a short break, I made my way to the pre-op holding area to check on my patient. I pushed the button on the wall and the doors swished open. Dozens of patients lay on stretchers, separated by striped curtains, anxiously awaiting their turn for surgery. Doctors and nurses checked charts and vital signs while monitors beeped and alarmed, and IV fluids dripped rhythmically.

Before I could locate my patient, a blond-haired toddler ran out of the pediatric holding area toward me. His blue eyes matched his pajamas. He giggled. As his parents called out, "Matthew, come back!" he ran to me at full speed. I caught him as he jumped, locking my neck in a tight embrace.

He cuddled his face to mine, squeezing his little legs around my waist. I felt his heart pound against my chest and rocked him back and forth. His parents apologized as they tried to pry Matthew off me.

I had a difficult time letting go, and said, "Thank you, Matthew, you made it worthwhile coming in to work today." The words to the song came back to me, "He will hold you in His arms."

To my surprise, Matthew was my patient. I interviewed his parents regarding his surgery, allergies, and other medical questions. I could see the anxiety in their eyes and attempted to soothe their fears with words of encouragement, but I knew that their relief would only come when they saw Matthew safe and sound in the recovery area.

The surgeon approached me, and with a smile said, "Open your hand."

He placed a gold-colored coin on my palm. "Someone gave this to me this morning and asked me to pass it on. Now I give it to you to pass on."

The inscription on the coin read, "Peace I give you."

I turned to my patient's mother and placed the coin in her clammy hand.

She reluctantly handed Matthew back into my arms.

I walked toward OR 21 with Matthew hugging my neck softly.

My prayer was answered. It was a peaceful day after all.

Ivani Greppi

Chimes in the Snow

*M*usic *has charms to soothe the savage breast,*
to soften rocks, or bend a knotted oak.

William Congreve

"That boy's going to die and he knows it," said one of
the other nurses. "Look at his eyes. Why can't they do
something?"

I'd been looking into those eyes for days. Twelve-year-
old John had a ruptured appendix with major complications, not something we expected to kill a child with the
kind of antibiotics available. But he continued to deteriorate, gangrene set in, and the smell of death crept in, in
spite of all our efforts.

I glanced out of the ICU window. All I saw was a strange,
gray world with little color except the narrow houses
smashed next to other tall, narrow houses perched on the
edge of steep hills. The houses looked as if they'd tumble
down with the slightest wind from a passing cardinal's
wing. Clouds stretched across the sky like dirty rags.

It was the late 1970s and my husband, Karl, had taken a

new job as a respiratory therapist in Butler, Pennsylvania. We moved ourselves and children across the country from the north Texas prairie to a small industrial steel town, and I went to work in the local hospital.

At first I loved the hills, being from flat land, and the tree colors during Indian summer made me want to get out paints and capture everything on canvas. But snow came in October, and it never left. Streets turned black and gray as the city sprinkled coal dust on the snow for traction. I missed the wide-open, warm Texas skies.

And I dreaded going to work.

Tension laced through the ICU like we'd all been caught in a net. Our young patient's parents and physician had the same glazed looks of disbelief that said, "How can this be happening? Why is this happening?" and the unspoken question, "How can God not help him?" We had strict visiting rules in the ICU at that time, but we broke them all, letting his parents stay around the clock.

The entire staff of the ICU took turns staying with John and his parents so that a nurse was at his bedside, touching his hand at all times. John's parents looked at us with eyes that asked, "What can we do? What did we do wrong?"

Every time I looked at John, I saw my son, Jeff, almost the same age. I pictured Jeff sick and me helpless. I could hardly stand it.

Other nurses felt the same way. We tried not to get too involved with our patients; the emotional toll could be too great. But detachment didn't always work.

"I'll come in early; I can't sleep anyway."

"Tom has to work this evening, I can stay late with John." Some nurses volunteered to work past their time to leave and others came in early. We couldn't stand the idea of leaving him alone and we were frustrated by our inability to change the situation.

John didn't make it, in spite of our efforts. He died at 5:00 PM and I worked the rest of my shift on autopilot. The normal back-and-forth bantering that keeps the ICU tension at bay died with John. All of us worked, doing what we had to do, saying little.

As medical professionals we knew we couldn't save all of our patients. But death should have exceptions. It should never come for children.

I can't keep doing this, I thought. *The ICU is too hard. It's like I watch my own children die over and over.*

I walked home that night, seeing a gray world, trapped hundreds of miles from family, smothered by hills that closed in more tightly each day.

Just as I reached our little blue house, music rang out from the small church across the street. That seemed strange. The chimes never played at night. I turned around when I reached the top of the stairs to the porch. Just as I looked at the church, a full moon slipped from behind the ragged clouds and lit the snow with a blinding glow. The light glinted from the stained-glass windows and shone off the cross on the steeple. Stars winked between the clouds.

I wasn't deserted and neither was John or his family. God was with them and with me. I had to accept life as it was, full of hope and of mystery, things we'd never understand. I'd found new eyes by which to view my world.

Gazing around, I saw the beauty in the snow, the hills, and in God's plan. It's there if we look for it . . . in the flash of a bird's wing, the smile of a child, and in the sound of a chime.

Over the next forty years of nursing, when my sight got clouded again—and it did—I simply listened for the chimes in the snow and my vision became clear.

Carol Shenold

The Lifeline

Words have a longer life than deeds.

Pindar

Michelle baffled the doctors. Her symptoms were vague and subjective—weakness, fatigue, tingling, dizziness. They could indicate any number of disease processes. Or none. "Most likely it's psychosomatic," her internist said, but he admitted her to the hospital for tests and observation anyway.

Michelle had been raped a year earlier and had just found out she would soon have to testify in her rapist's trial. That's when the symptoms had begun. After her tests came back negative, her doctor prepared to discharge her from the hospital.

Then Michelle stopped breathing.

The resuscitation team intubated the young woman and rushed her to intensive care. Her limbs lay limp and useless on the bed. She was dependent on the ventilator to fill her lungs with life-sustaining oxygen. At first, Michelle was able to nod and shake her head when the nurses asked her questions. By the time I was assigned to care for her, she could only blink her eyes—twice for yes, once for no.

"It could be Reye's syndrome," conjectured her neurologist, but at twenty-six, Michelle was well beyond the usual age range for that malady. More than once, the doctors rejected a diagnosis of Guillain-Barré syndrome, but when further tests proved inconclusive, they finally settled on that diagnosis. The pulmonary doctor inserted a tracheostomy tube. Michelle would be on the ventilator for a long time.

I worked as a straight 11-7 nurse, and our shift was usually quiet. This gave me extra time to spend with Michelle, and we quickly developed our routine. Each night I asked, "Would you like me to swab your mouth?" Blink, blink. "Do you want an extra pillow under your head?" Blink. "Would you like to turn on your side?" Blink, blink. As I washed her face or combed her hair, I told Michelle about the weather outside her windowless room or gave updates on the antics of my new puppy. Without a word on her part, we formed a bond, Michelle and I.

All too soon came the terrible night when the blinking stopped. "She can't move her eyes at all," the evening nurse said. "I'm afraid we're losing her."

After report, I inserted drops and taped her eyelids shut to protect her precious corneas. Michelle was now completely trapped inside a body that would not respond to the simplest command. Her lifeline was gone.

Days stretched into weeks, and Michelle's condition remained the same. I talked to her in hopes that she could still hear me and performed range of motion exercises to keep her joints from stiffening into permanent contractures.

In December, Michelle's parents decorated her room in a festive atmosphere, and we allowed them to stay beyond regular visiting hours to celebrate with her.

Christmas came and went. Still no response.

After the holidays, Michelle developed a urinary tract infection and pneumonia. We battled all the familiar foes that attack a comatose patient, even one as young as Michelle. Once her body overcame the infections, her heart rate began to soar, and she perspired profusely. I had seen those same signs in patients with severe brain damage.

"I don't think she'll ever wake up," I quietly confessed to another nurse during shift change one morning. "It's been eleven weeks now."

"I know," she replied. "I've never seen a patient stay in ICU so long."

That morning I left with a heavy heart. The thought that Michelle would not recover and the fact that she was so near my age haunted me. Even the prospect of a two-week vacation did nothing to cheer me as images of Michelle's taped eyes and motionless body flickered across my mind.

When I returned from my much-needed break, things were hopping in my assigned unit. Lisa, the 3–11 nurse, was snowed under with two patients in crisis at once, so I pitched in and began taking vital signs and doing neuro checks. As I sat at the desk completing my nurse's notes on one patient, I heard a gravelly voice call, "Tracy?"

"What?" I asked, still busy charting.

"Tracy?" the voice called again. It sounded as if it came from the hall outside our unit. *Someone must be playing a trick on me,* I thought. *I don't have time for games.*

"What is it?" I asked, a bit more irritated this time, and stepped into the hall.

"Tracy!" That's when I realized the disembodied voice came from Michelle's room. I ran to her side.

"You're awake!" I cried, always the perceptive one.

Michelle smiled. "They took my trach out today. The doctor said I probably wouldn't be able to talk for a while, but I needed help. Could you please turn me on my side?"

"Sure thing," I said and moved her emaciated body, tucking pillows behind her back. "But how did you know I was here?"

"Lisa told me you were coming on," Michelle replied, "and I heard you talking to the patient in the next room. I remembered your voice."

Though she did not remember much from the weeks she was paralyzed, Michelle remembered my voice. When her body forsook her and she was unable even to blink an eye, I thought her lifeline was gone. But Michelle latched on to the thread that had formed between us, a thread that became stronger the more I talked to her.

Michelle recovered over the next few weeks, slowly regaining use of her long-forgotten muscles. Eventually, she resumed a normal life.

My transformation took place more quickly as I realized the power of the spoken word and the lifeline those words can create.

Tracy Crump

My Name Is John

Shut out all of your past except that which will help you weather your tomorrows.

Sir William Osler

"Hello. My name is John . . . and I'm an alcoholic." That's the first thing they taught us in rehab—to admit it. But here I am, after being dry for over a year, in the hospital. My relapse was bad.

I watched a guy in scrubs pass my door. He'd gone down the hallway a couple of times already. He was always smiling and had a certain bounce to his step. Finally, my courage built, I waited for him to pass again.

"Pssst. Pssst," I tried to get his attention. He peeked his head into my doorway.

"Yes sir?" he offered. "John?"

"Yeah man, it's me," I answered hoarsely.

"John?" He quizzed again, as the truth was sinking in.

He stood at the foot of my bed, the reality hitting him in the face.

It hit me too as I looked at this man dressed in scrubs.

He was clean, healthy, and a sparkle decorated his eyes. He stood taller and more confidently than when I first met him.

He had been in the rehab group I lead.

Together, we had encouraged the guys in our group—to be strong, to face our problems, with God and not the bottle. We had helped other friends when they were close to relapsing. We talked them through the pain—emotionally and physically. One time, a friend had lost his wife and family and was missing them so terribly he was going to hit the bottle again. We stayed by his side all day and into the evening, playing Frisbee at the park, riding bikes, bowling, drinking coffee. We stayed with him until the sorrow passed.

The two of us had found purpose for our lives again.

There in that hospital bed, with tubes hooked up to me, fighting to breathe through the pain in my body, I realized I had lost my purpose.

And here before me was a man who radiated his.

"John," he said again. "Man, I've been thinking about you. What's been going on?" He pulled up a chair close to me and unlike most men, this friend took my hand in his.

Tears trickled down my face, wetting the pillow. *What did he have that I didn't?* Or did I have it and lose it?

My friend kept talking—about things in our past and things in his life now. He explained that he was in school and striving to become an R.N. He had passion about his life. I wanted what he had but I didn't know if I would live to ever have it. My liver had shut down. I was in bad shape.

He knew. I knew it. "John, you look awful."

I had to laugh. He was always a straight shooter. None of us ever wondered where we were with him. If he was mad, he told us, got it over with, and moved on. He was fair.

"Yeah, I know."

"Live the lessons, John. You had a relapse but that's not the end, you know. But man, you gotta do it for yourself—not your wife, your kids, your family—but yourself. Let me help you."

I knew he would, too. He had become a man of his word.

We talked that week I was in the hospital. We talked a lot. He shared how he hadn't always been true to his word. He told me about those he had hurt in the process—those he had lost. I liked this man—he was vulnerable and shared openly. He wasn't afraid of what I might think.

During that week I realized so many of my insecurities. I faced my emotional pain and it was hell. But my friend was there for me. He visited during his rounds and he stayed after his shift. We laughed together and cried together.

And one more time, for one more day, because of the man in the scrubs, I am dry.

John
as told to Kelly Martindale

New Life

*H*ope *is tomorrow's veneer over today's disappointment.*

Evan Esar

"A baby was born last night!"

The nurse, a fellow relief worker, shared this amazing news with a look of pure joy on her face. We rarely heard good news in Banda Aceh, Indonesia, during the weeks following the December 2004 earthquake and tsunami, so her announcement was greeted with smiles all around. We all agreed to go to the local hospital together to visit the new family.

Along with my fellow relief workers, I looked forward to a scene of joy within the walls of a hospital. Thus far hospitals were only reminders of how much was lost, because for every person saved and recovering in a bed, there were multiple stories of heartache for their family members swept away by the waves.

I had traveled to the island of Sumatra, Indonesia, from my home in Phoenix, Arizona, in February 2005 to train relief workers on trauma and to help survivors. As a mental health therapist, I had seen firsthand how worn thin the relief workers were by the constant grief and loss surrounding them. After being in Indonesia for several weeks, I was feeling a little worn myself. We all needed an uplifting moment of hope.

We made our way to the hospital, walking toward the nondescript building with excitement. Pausing before entering, my eyes lingered on the wall before me and I stopped.

Stretched across the entire length of the hospital wall were signs, each one displaying the word *dicari,* which means "looking for" in Indonesian. Underneath that phrase was the face, name, and description of a missing family member. Some signs had just one photograph and description, but far too many showed a couple, several very young children, or even an entire family. Some signs were black and white, old and faded by the elements and hanging on by just a corner. Others looked professionally printed, the colors still bright, the sign still firmly affixed to the wall.

As I looked at that wall, I grieved for the hope on display. The hope the people who created and hung those signs held for finding their loved ones. Week by week, it had become increasingly clear how unlikely a happy ending would be in this tragic situation.

Standing there, I felt the weight of my experience thus far. The stories the survivors shared with me echoed in my ears. The father who told me, "I lost my wife and four children to the water and I have never found their bodies." The disbelieving mother who cried, "My baby, only a few months old, was torn from my grip when I was in the tsunami." The priest who lamented, "I did not do more to save those around me. I forgot that waves follow earthquakes. How could I forget?" I grieved with them all.

Shaking off the memories for now, I continued past the grim reminder of hope and loss, looking forward to a more hopeful scene inside. Then, walking into the hospital, we heard the word. The baby had died. I never learned the reason, but saw the tiny bundle in the corner of the room. Wrapped in a blue blanket with a pattern of hearts and teddy bears, the small form served as another reminder of how closely death lingered even six weeks after the disaster. I felt the urge to leave the hospital with its stories of sadness and the evidence of loss papering the front. But where would I go? Sadness and destruction were everywhere in Banda Aceh.

Then, an Indonesian nurse dressed in a crisp white uniform approached us. She wore a white scarf covering her hair, as is traditional for Muslim Indonesian women. Her smile warmed my heart. Despite the tragedy that surrounded her and having to walk by the wall of missing people every day, she still radiated joy in serving others. With her bright smile, she brought us into a room and showed us twin newborn infants swaddled in matching blankets.

Laying side by side, only their tiny red faces peeked out. I noticed that the blankets had the same pattern of hearts and teddy bears as the other infant's swaddling. These children, born to a survivor of the tsunami that very day, showed all of us how hope endures in the midst of tragedy. One young life lost, but two lives started that day in the hospital. Gazing down on them, I felt renewed by such a strong reminder that life does indeed go on.

"Congratulations," I said to the family gathered around. The exhausted mother only smiled, but her mother, the proud grandmother of the babies, told us, "The nurses made the babies live." In a time and place with very limited medical resources and many potential complications of childbirth, the nurses had ushered in new life against great odds.

Then my friend offered to take my photograph with three of the nurses working that day. In the photo, initially you see only our differences. I am a Christian, American man. They are Muslim, Indonesian women. My height towers over their small frames. Looking closer, though, you see that what unifies us is our smiles. Initially brought together because of disaster, we now celebrated new life together.

Their smiles and joy remind me to this day that hope lives, even in the midst of tragedy.

Thomas Winkel

[EDITORS' NOTE: *To learn more about supporting tsunami relief, go to www.WordPointPublishing.com.*]

Sustained Me

You will sustain him on his sickbed.

Psalm 41:3

You were present at my son's birth. Cheering me on.
Telling me not to give up. Refusing to take a break.
Certain that my baby would be here any minute.
Your badge, "Registered Nurse," was pinned fittingly
   over your heart.
A few hours later . . .
Still, you were there.
Things had taken a turn for the worse . . .
Vacuum extractor . . . forceps . . .
You held one of my hands while my husband held the
   other.
Our baby was born blue, deprived of oxygen.
How I longed to hear him make a sound.
A team of twenty-five assembled in the birthing room,
   there to give life to our child.
APGAR—one—not good.
I knew this, but refused to let it register.

Hot tears stung my face, but my baby had yet to cry.
Suctioning . . . establishing an airway.
How could one so tiny require the care of so many?
The team worked feverishly as our baby teetered
　precariously between life and death.
Finally . . . that first glorious cry! A sound I shall never
　forget.
"Take a quick peek," they said as they wheeled him off to
　the NICU.
"He's in good hands," you promised.
I knew it was all you could say.
It was the only thing you were sure of.
You comforted me while my husband accompanied our
　firstborn son to the nursery.
Several hours later, I caught my first glimpse of him . . .
　big, rosy, and beautiful
All nine pounds, six ounces of him stuffed into his
　Isolette.
Attached to wires and tubes and needles.
There you were again, different in your appearance,
Yet somehow the same.
A different name on your badge, but the words
　"Registered Nurse," positioned like your colleague's,
　suitably over your heart.
You tended to his every need. You even tended to mine.
I held my baby for the first time . . . dressed in scrubs and
　gloves.
It wasn't supposed to be like this. I choked back tears,
　grateful that I could hold him.
A million thoughts ran through my head. *What lies ahead*
　for this child? Will there be learning disabilities, visual prob-
　lems . . . or worse?
The "what-ifs" were too much to bear. But it didn't matter.
I loved him with a fierceness I could not describe.

"Get some rest," you told me. "We'll take good care of him
   here. We'll ring your room if there are any problems."
You snapped a Polaroid picture of him for me, his tiny
   fingers grasping my gloved hand.
I clung to that picture.
I fell asleep, clutching it to my heart.
Medical specialists and machines sustained my son's life.
You sustained my spirit.
How, I wondered, *does nursing school ever prepare someone for
   these things?*
Then I realized that nursing school, despite everything it
   teaches you, could never really train you for this.
For this is truly the work of angels on earth.

                                             Wendy Young

Optimistic Light

Let your light shine. Shine within you so that it can shine on someone else. Let your light shine.

Oprah Winfrey

I survived a brain stem stroke and my future dwells in dark shadows. I am a ventilator-dependent quadriplegic. All I can do is lay here. I wish for death . . . complete darkness.

I hear two nurses talking in hushed tones. An alarm buzzes. "It's just room number 120. He's always pushing his call button."

The younger nurse asks, "Should I go check on him?"

"No, he's fine. He probably just wants to gripe about something. He's just a difficult patient."

"If you're sure . . . " she says doubtfully.

The disturbing conversation stops as my family walks into the room. In the past three weeks, I had been diagnosed with spinal meningitis, had a cardiac and respiratory arrest, stroked at the brain stem, and been deemed brain-dead. The ravages of worry are stamped on their pale faces.

The nurses' words lurk in my head, and I hear them again and again when my family leaves to get lunch. I'm alone. I am terrified, but cannot speak and have no way to tell anyone. I don't think I'm a difficult patient, as they defined that other man. I hope the nurse responds to my ventilator alarms. *What happens if my ventilator hose pops off? Will someone come running? They ignored another's alarms, will they ignore mine?*

Alone . . . all alone. The ventilator is my sole companion. I count the seconds between each breath. One, two, three, four, five, six, air in, air out. One, two, three, four, five, six, air in, air out . . . over and over I count. *It took longer to get a breath!* No, I just don't always count at the same rate. Panic stirs in my chest. *What happens if the machine doesn't supply a burst of air?* Another breath eases my trepidation.

A new nurse, Mary, takes care of me all week. The anxiety builds each day as the sun sinks lower in the sky. *Will that other nurse, who thinks I'm a pest, be on duty tomorrow?* At night I lay awake and agonize. Each day as Mary greets me, I breathe a mental sigh of relief.

Tomorrow arrives and Mary ushers in a new day. She talks to me even though I can't talk back. She is five-foot nothing, if that, with a bouncy, upbeat personality that makes people instantly like her the minute she bebops into the room. Just watching her check my blood pressure, temperature, and arrange my pillows lightens my spirits.

If only I could tell her about the conversation I overheard.

After a week of virtual isolation, Mary introduces me and my family to an alphabet chart. She knows I can't move or talk and empathizes with how lonely, boring, and frustrating it is for me—lying by as conversation flies around me.

Mary teases me, "Your days of daydreaming are over. Your family may enjoy your silence, but today that is all over. By blinking your eyes you can start telling *them* what to do and how." She winks conspiratorially.

Mary explains the method to help me communicate with the chart. "Someone holds up the chart and points to each letter." She demonstrates as she instructs. "To say, 'Hi,' they point to A, B, C, D, E, F, G, and at H, you'll blink. They follow the same process for the letter I—A, B, C, D, E, F, G, H, and at I, you'll blink. Anytime you want to say a word, just use the board. If someone asks you a yes or no question, you answer with one blink for yes and two blinks for no. Any questions?"

Now, I can tell someone my fear.

I blink once to indicate yes, I have a question.

"Ask away."

I spell out. "Can I ask not to get a nurse?"

"Sure." Mary raises her bushy eyebrows. "Why?"

Painstakingly, I recount the conversation between that horrible nurse and the trainee.

"I'll take care of it, don't you worry. You know most nurses don't feel that way or act like that." Mary's right. I never experience any such instances with any other nurses.

The shadow of despair recedes under the light of Mary's competent and kind ministrations. I don't have to face each day with apprehension or wonder if I will get that nurse or anyone like her again.

I spell words and construct sentences in this fashion all during the day when my family's around. They stick close to me after I share that story, except when visitors come. They can stretch their legs and take a breather during those times or anytime Mary is on duty.

Mary is my most frequent visitor. Each day she works, she perches on my bed and chats with me on her breaks, because she wants my company. I think I get far more from these conversations than she does. The time given freely makes me feel normal. I am more than something to be pitied. I'm not just a patient. I am her friend. She gets two fifteen-minute breaks a day and she spends them with me. Most days she comes and talks during part of her lunch with me, too. Mary stays with me days and encourages others to use the board, but the nights leave me in silence.

Mary stays late after her shift and teaches the night shift how to use the board. I miss Mary at night, but another nurse watches me closely and talks to me in her down-time. Hours elapse. My family is at home. With the free time on my hands, in the darkness I think about what my future holds.

Before Mary's morning break, I ask my mother about my condition and she explains it the best she can. "You have locked-in syndrome."

I spell, "What does that mean?"

The color drains from her face. Her features crumple and tears spill down her cheeks. She fortifies herself with a deep breath and spews out the answer. "It means you will never move anything but your eyes, nor breathe without a ventilator, nor eat by mouth, nor speak."

Mary pops into my room while Mom explains this to me. "Sounds pretty hopeless, doesn't it? Well it isn't. I've researched what they can do at the rehabs. They're going to teach you a bunch. You can control all kinds of things with your eyes, like a computer, your television, radio, and all kinds of other stuff. You won't walk and talk, but you can still do a lot of things. We just need to get you well enough to go to the rehab. You're going to be a busy lady."

Leave it to Mary to shine an optimistic light on the challenges ahead.

More nurses like Mary take care of me throughout my rehabilitation. They are all a blessing, but Mary is special. She chased away the darkness with a ray of hope, when I had none.

Jessica Kennedy

10

THANK YOU

If the only prayer you ever say in your whole life is "thank you," that would suffice.

Meister Eckhart

God Supplies Angels

Therefore my heart is glad and my glory rejoices; my flesh will also rest in hope.

Psalm 16:9

I lay flat on my back staring at the ceiling. It was late at night, and I could see shadows from the nurses' station shining through the glass door into my room. I could hear the beeping of the machines around me. Each time I inhaled, I breathed in the horrible smell of the yellow Xeroform bandages that covered my raw, burned skin. I had been in a major motor home fire, and I was 48 percent burned. My back was shattered and broken. Within seconds, my life had been dismantled. My husband had a 9 percent chance of living and was just two doors away from me in the unit. I missed him so much and did not want to live without him.

Each night was like the night before, lying and waiting for the night nurse to come in and hurt me with the two-hour bandage change. My depression and anxiety continued to grow. Nighttime seemed the worst time. I could not sleep, and my thoughts ran amok with dogged doubt and little hope.

I remember one night vividly. My finger did a yo-yo motion with the call button. I did not want to bother the nurses, but I did need to talk to someone. The burn unit is busy, and one of the hardest in which to work. However, my emotional pain won the battle and I rang. One of the night nurses, Joan, entered my room. She was a tall, thin woman in her fifties who usually worked days. I was so glad to see her. She always called me her prize patient, and she listened to me when she had time.

"What's going on with you tonight?" she asked. "Are you in pain? Why aren't you asleep?"

"Asleep" was a post-traumatic trigger word for me. I was asleep when the accident happened, so I rarely slept now. Somehow in my emotional state, I thought the accident would not have occurred if I had been awake. So, in my drug-induced stupor I felt I needed to be on night duty, so I could be in control. When a person is burned, all four parts that make up our humanhood is affected: emotional, spiritual, physical, and intellectual. Each is damaged and needs to be healed. My pain was continual, and the fear of going to sleep, no matter what drugs they gave me, was impossible to shake.

As Joan stood in front of me, I noticed the pretty, gold, shiny earrings she was wearing. I started to share with her some of my fears of looking like a monster.

"Will anyone accept me the way I look now?"

Joan pulled a chair over beside me and listened.

"Will I ever be normal again, or pretty, or able to walk?" I sobbed. "Will this pain ever go away? Will I be able to feed myself and put pretty earrings on again?"

Abruptly, Joan stopped me. "Have you looked at your face yet?" she asked.

"No, I am afraid to," I cried.

She immediately got up and left the room. I feared what was going to happen next.

As Joan reentered the room, she had a mirror in her hand. "No!" I shouted. "I am afraid to look!" I had seen my arms and legs during the bandage change and I knew I looked like a freak.

She came closer to me and started to brush my hair, quietly saying, "You are pretty. Your face is all right. It is rosy with first-degree burns but that will go away." Then she took her earrings off and clipped them on to my ears. My tears gushed uncontrollably as I found the courage to look in the mirror.

For five weeks I had wondered what my face looked like; now I knew. Thanks to a nurse named Joan who took the time to listen and help me through this important transition, I now had hope. All would be well someday.

Susan Lugli

[EDITOR'S NOTE: *Susan adds, "After six years and numerous plastic surgeries, the love of my life is back to normal, working as he did before the accident. We are thankful for each day we have together."*]

To School Nurses

All us kids think you are swell.
You care for us when we're not well.
You give us icepacks for our heads.
You let us rest on little beds.
You give us tissues for our nose.
And check for splinters in our toes.
When we fall and break a bone,
You call our moms on the phone.
Our pierced ears you disinfect,
When infection you suspect.
If we bring notes, you give us pills,
To cure all our assorted ills.
You help us when our throats are sore,
And when we throw up on the floor.
When we're hot, you take our temps.
You never make us feel like wimps.
You show us that you really care.
School is better 'cause you are there.

Ellen Javernick

Angels of Mercy

Gratitude is born in hearts that take time to count up past mercies.

Charles E. Jefferson

My aunts, uncles, and cousins had come to our house for our annual Thanksgiving dinner in 1945. Our day was filled with plenty of good food and lots of laughter.

I was five years old, playing in the basement, when I fell off a twelve-inch-high step stool onto my back. My sister ran upstairs to the kitchen to get Mom. I wasn't moving. Mom helped me up the steps and sat me on a chair to observe me. Noticing that I was turning yellow and blue, she quickly got my uncle to help take me to Mercy Hospital in his car.

Snow was falling on an already white street, the stars twinkling in a black sky.

After serious discussion among several doctors, I was diagnosed with a ruptured spleen that had to be removed immediately. The doctors, machines, and lights frightened me. To this day I can recall the sights and sounds that permeated that small room.

And to add to my already heightened fear, my mom and dad were not permitted to stay in the emergency room with me. Medical technology and hospital practices were different back then. My mom had worn her heavy brown tweed coat. As I trembled on the examining table, I soon realized that if I threw my head back far enough, I could see her coat draped over a chair behind me. It was less scary then because I knew my mom would never leave me without putting her coat on; it was too cold outside.

"Twenty minutes and it would have been too late," I heard someone say.

In what seemed like a minute and an eternity, I woke up in an all-white hospital room with a big white bandage across my abdomen. White walls. White sheets. White pillows. When I look back on this, I can see a thin little girl drowning helplessly in a sea of white.

Throughout the three weeks I lay there in that hospital bed rallying for my life, nurses in white uniforms and white caps wandered in and out of my room. I didn't feel as terrified when they were there. They changed my bandages, changed my bedding, and washed my tiny body with their soft, gentle hands. They helped feed me.

As I got stronger, they let me be a little girl, encouraging me to play. Someone had generously given me a tube of red lipstick, which I used to adorn my lips, my cheeks, and the white sheets and pillowcases. When my mom noticed the red ribbons of color splashed everywhere, she apologized profusely to the nurses.

"Let her have fun," they insisted.

"Angels of mercy," my mom called them.

I welcomed them into my domain. Their freshly pressed white uniforms and caps stood out in my sea of white, like doves formed in the folds of God's clouds.

Since that snowy Thanksgiving night, my twenty allotted minutes to live have spanned more than five decades of life. I became a teacher, a writer, and best of all, a mother. I bandaged scraped knees, stayed up all night with stuffy noses, and made several visits to the emergency room with my children.

And each time I went through the double doors of an emergency room with one of my children's hands in mine, there were nurses to graciously greet me. Their white uniforms and white caps were no longer visible, but they were still like doves formed in the folds of God's clouds.

"Thank you," I whisper, recalling a snowy Thanksgiving night.

And I hear my mom say, "angels of mercy," her voice reaching me from the white light of heaven.

"Yes, Mom," I call back, looking up past the ceiling to the sky. "Angels of mercy."

Lola Di Giulio De Maci

To the Nurse Who Served in Vietnam

O Lord who lends me life, lend me a heart replete with thankfulness.

William Shakespeare

My name is Mike. I was a Marine, and I stepped on a mine during Operation Allenbrook. I lost both legs. You were my nurse who told me I was going home. You bathed me, kept me out of pain; you talked to me about beginning anew. It was not easy but you gave me hope. Today, I just retired. I have thought of you often . . . I don't even remember your name. I'll always remember your face.

My name is Roger. I was killed during a mortar attack in Plieku. You made sure all my personal effects made it home to my wife. I was there at night when you cried over all of us—praying for me and my family. Yes, God does care and He remembers you.

My name is Tan. I was a little child in Ban Me Thout, and you cared for me and helped me. I have leprosy. I was there when they took you away in the middle of the night.

I missed your singing to me. You were my missionary. My daughter has your name.

My name is Wayne. I was killed when our base camp got overrun at Bihn Phouc, but I remembered the times when you came to play games with us. You took my mind off the war; you made me forget. I was from Indiana. I told you that you reminded me of my girlfriend.

My name is Joe, and I am from Memphis. I rode on your plane coming over to Nam. You told me it was okay to be scared and you were going to pray for all of us. You took my last letter I wrote to my mom and dad and mailed it for me. I remember your perfume and your beautiful green eyes. I was killed by a mine that blew up my truck my first day.

My name is Jimmy. Me and all the guys want to thank you for a job well done. Please be easy on yourselves. Do you realize how many of us you saved? Do you know how many of us still have legs and arms that might have been removed if not for you? You helped ease our pain. You are the best and we appreciate all that you did. It was enough.

My name is David. I never got to tell you thanks for being there for me. For holding my hand and telling me I was going to be okay. Thanks for writing the letter to Mom; she told me how much she appreciated it when she got up here last year. Thank you for staying with me when I passed over. It is so beautiful here. I will be there for you when it is your time to come. I will call your name and I will hold your hand. I love you.

My name is Tony. My helicopter was shot down in the Plain of Reeds. I was on your burn ward. You wrote letters home for me. I told you that I loved you and you said all the guys said that to you. You don't understand—I still do.

Kerry Pardue

God's Hand

Never deprive someone of hope. It may be all they have.

H. Jackson Brown, Jr.

Somehow, it had all come to this.

A fifth-and-a-half-a-day drunk and drug addict, homeless in body and soul. Thirty-two years old, two failed suicide attempts. I'd lost everything. And everyone.

Then, on a night like countless others, in the unfurnished back room of someone's house, passed out on an old mattress on the floor, surrounded by unpacked boxes—something changed.

It had little to do with me. I had given up. Yet suddenly, in the silent hours before dawn, the world became perfectly still, and I was wide-awake, stone sober. A wailing came out of me, as a weight threatening to smother me crushed my body into the sheets, the tears pouring out of me like rain, like hard, deep, crystal cleansing rain until I could not breathe, could not see or hear or move, until whatever had been haunting me came rushing out with a shudder and a gasp and helpless hollow howling, and then died.

I was so sick in my spirit and body that much of what transpired the next few days following that night remains clouded in my mind, and I remember few details. I believe that I walked around in a stupor for a while, and those around me might have even suspected that the shattering of what was left of my sanity had finally come, because no one really spoke to me much. I know that I considered taking a drink, because I no longer knew how to go through a day without doing so, but that somehow I did not. I was too weak to understand what it meant, or what step I should take next.

Still, I had surrendered. On a primitive and very human level, I had given up, and given in. I had, in some unfathomable way, chosen *life*. I was far too sick and confused at the time to rationally think any of this, of course, to be able to reason such an unreasonable thing. But God's grace was sufficient. I actually went one day, then another, without drinking. His helpless, but willing and obedient child again, the miracle had begun.

Sometime later, on a gray and rainy afternoon, I found my way to the downtown mission, to an AA meeting in the basement of an old stone church. I don't remember much about that first visit, or even exactly how I got there. But one moment will remain in my mind as long as I live. I can still see my hands shaking badly as I tried to pour a cup of coffee, the stuff spilling all over the table, and a wrinkled hand reaching in to gently steady the cup and pour it full. And I remember those eyes, the eyes of this seventy-three-year-old woman, and I saw peace in them.

"Looks like you could use some help," she said.

Her name was Margaret. She told me she was "seventy-something, and that's all you need to know." She had been a widow for eight years, and in recovery from her alcoholism for six. And for whatever reason, she took it upon herself to be my angel.

Margaret had been a nurse all her professional life. After she retired, when her husband of forty years became bedridden with cancer, he asked her to take care of him at home, and of course she did.

Margaret came to every AA meeting held in the mission. She had at some point taken on the responsibility of arriving early and making the coffee. She was happiest when helping; a servant's heart beat strong within her.

Every time I tried to run away, emotionally or physically, Margaret would know. She could see the look in my eyes, and see what was happening. She knew this familiar fear personally, and did not take it lightly. She allowed me no self-pity, no easy way out. And her gentle strength helped save my life.

In a sense, Margaret became Christ to me, much like my own grandmother had when I was a child. Growing up in my alcoholic home, I found refuge in my Mamaw's house, her unconditional love wrapping itself around me like a quilt. I had over the years nearly forgotten this place. Now Margaret's love felt the same.

Margaret embodied a kind of calm against my longing. She knew how to listen. I had over the years learned to trust no one. Yet, in a matter of days, I risked drawing near a place shining within her that felt at long last like home. Perhaps, somewhere deep in her nurse's soul, she possessed a gift of healing that went far beyond her physical years of professional service. Because for one exhausted, shameful man, her eyes shared a dancing grace, and her hands held a healing that time can never still.

I knew her for three brief years. She hadn't told me about her cancer until months after we met. Others knew, as it turned out, but she had asked that the truth be kept from me, at least for a little while, perhaps until I had gotten stronger. To the end, she tended to my needs rather than her own.

I've been clean and sober for over seventeen years. In all that time, I've had to learn to move from my selfishness into a spirit of giving, of sharing the hope that Margaret and many others shared with me on a cold afternoon that now seems forever ago. Margaret is gone, but has of course never left me. Whenever fear and shame and an old but familiar sense of loneliness creep into my soul, there remains the soft brush of her hand across my cheek . . . a mother's hand . . . God's hand . . . a nurse's hand.

James E. Robinson

Knowing Your Limits

To oblige one grateful man, I will oblige a great many who are not so.

Lucius Annaeus Seneca

As a physician assistant, I spent the first two years after graduating at one of the largest correctional facilities in the New York City area, Rikers Island.

Staff members rotated through the various clinics, infirmary, and special housing units addressing the many medical needs of our inmates. It was in the women's mental health unit that I met Renee.

Renee was a disheveled woman in her midtwenties, with long matted hair, dirty clothing, and a toothless smile. During my daily rounds to the unit, she stood in close proximity, grinning and drooling, and making bizarre gestures. She often attempted to communicate, but her speech was incoherent and tangential. Abused by family and most people who came in contact with her, Renee had a lifelong history of schizophrenia and depression. She had been in countless psychiatric programs and on various medications. Too often she became noncompliant and relapsed into a world of paranoia where she self-medicated with illicit drugs.

Now she was in jail for transporting cocaine. She was apprehended carrying a suitcase full while doing a "favor for a friend." This was a most unfortunate incident because Renee was not capable of understanding her actions. Her medical condition prevented her from making sound judgments. She would have gladly carried a lit stick of dynamite had it been offered to her.

She'd been assessed by our mental health team and placed on multiple antipsychotic medications, but her condition never improved. Because our facility was over-crowded and our staff overburdened, we were unable to provide the intensive follow-up she desperately needed. After many weeks of treatment failure, she was transferred to an inpatient psychiatric hospital that was better equipped to assess and treat her. I felt so sad letting her go, and regretted that we were limited in doing more for her.

Several months later the time rolled around for me to rotate through the mental health ward again. One morning as I entered the unit, I was approached by a neatly dressed young woman with a coiffed brown bob, sparkling white teeth, and a pretty smile.

"Do you remember me?" she asked.

"No, I'm sorry, I don't."

"It's me, Renee!"

Excitedly she told me about her stay at the psychiatric hospital where she had been thoroughly assessed and treated. With medication adjustments, her thought process and speech became coherent. Then the staff could focus on her physical well-being. She cut her hair, bathed, was fitted for dentures, and given new clothing. Now she functioned like an average person and was preparing for her trial with the competence she needed.

"Thank you," she said, with confidence and poise.

"Thank you?" I asked, somewhat stunned. "I always regretted that we couldn't do more for you—that we let you down."

She smiled easily. "No. Your team admitted your boundaries and transferred me to a team of specialists who worked a miracle. Thank you."

Frank Serigano

Thanking Ruby

I knew I wanted to be a nurse at a very young age, and at the ripe old age of eighteen I graduated from LPN school. I thought I knew everything about everything!

My first job was as charge nurse of two floors of a large nursing home. My day consisted of giving medications and changing dressings. I was completely overwhelmed. Imagine how intimidated I was to be in charge of a middle-aged woman who had been giving patient care since before I was born. Ruby was probably forty-five or fifty, which at the time seemed very old to me. There were many times I would have to ask her how I should do something. She always said, "Girl, you are so green."

Ruby took me under her wing; I learned more nursing skills from that woman than I learned in school. Ruby always touched patients when she talked to them and asked them how they were feeling. I think what struck me the most about Ruby was the way she cared for the unresponsive patients. She took such care in cleaning them when they had soiled themselves. She talked to them gently the whole time. And God help the person who was less than kind to one of Ruby's patients—and they were *all* Ruby's patients. There were many times I heard her say her famous line, "This is someone's mother or father."

I stayed at that job for about a year and I left without thanking Ruby because at the time I didn't comprehend how much she had taught me. Remember, I knew it all. I went on to work in several other areas before landing in dialysis twenty-one years ago. I had worked there about ten or twelve years when we got a new patient who had, besides renal failure, end-stage cancer. Bertha R. Johnson weighed about ninety pounds.

One afternoon, she was incontinent while on the dialysis machine. One of the new nurses and I took her to the bathroom to get her cleaned up, and it was obvious my coworker was disgusted with the situation. I sent her away and told her I would clean Bertha.

As I was washing her, I said, "Mrs. Johnson, I am so sorry if she made you feel embarrassed. She's new."

She replied, "Oh, girl, she's still green. She will learn. And why don't you call me Ruby?"

I could not believe my ears! I said, "Oh my gosh, Ruby Johnson! You used to work at the Clover Hill nursing home in 1977, didn't you?"

She smiled with pride. "Girl, I worked in that place until I got too sick with this cancer. Why?"

"It's me. Jacqueline!" I said. Then as we reminisced, I finally got a chance to thank Ruby for her kindness and all that she had taught me.

Ruby laughed. "You were so green, but it looks like I taught you well," she said, patting my hand.

I gently dried her face. "Indeed you did."

Jacqueline Gray Carrico

Thank You for Your Care

It must be very hard at times
To do all that you do;
To serve others so unselfishly
While "thank-yous" are so few.

You work long hours and yet you smile
While giving needed care.
I've seen concern within your eyes,
And kindness, deep and rare.

You choose to go that extra mile
When you know you are needed;
The virtuous call of nursing
You have truly heeded.

Thanks for all you did for me
While I was in your care;
You'll be remembered in my heart,
And each and every prayer.

Denise A. Dewald

Who Is Jack Canfield?

Jack Canfield is the cocreator and editor of the Chicken Soup for the Soul series, which *Time* magazine has called "the publishing phenomenon of the decade." The series includes more than 140 titles with over 100 million copies in print in forty-seven languages. Jack is also the coauthor of eight other bestselling books, including *The Success Principles™: How to Get from Where You Are to Where You Want to Be, Dare to Win, The Aladdin Factor, You've Got to Read This Book,* and *The Power of Focus: How to Hit Your Business, Personal and Financial Targets with Absolute Certainty.*

Jack has recently developed a telephone coaching program and an online coaching program based on his most recent book, *The Success Principles.* He also offers a seven-day Breakthrough to Success seminar every summer, which attracts 400 people from about fifteen countries around the world.

Jack is the CEO of Chicken Soup for the Soul Enterprises and the Canfield Training Group in Santa Barbara, California, and is founder of the Foundation for Self-Esteem in Culver City, California. He has conducted intensive personal and professional development seminars on the principles of success for more than a million people in twenty-nine countries around the world. Jack is a dynamic keynote speaker, and he has spoken to hundreds of thousands at more than 1,000 corporations, universities, professional conferences, and conventions and has been seen by millions more on national television shows such as *Oprah, Montel, The Today Show, Larry King Live, Fox and Friends, Inside Edition, Hard Copy, CNN's Talk Back Live, 20/20, Eye to Eye,* and the *NBC Nightly News* and the *CBS Evening News.* Jack was also a featured teacher in the hit movie *The Secret.*

Jack is the recipient of many awards and honors, including three honorary doctorates and a Guinness World Records Certificate for having seven books from the Chicken Soup for the Soul series appearing on the *New York Times* bestseller list on May 24, 1998.

To write to Jack or for inquiries about Jack as a speaker, his coaching programs, trainings, or seminars, use the following contact information:

Jack Canfield
The Canfield Companies
P.O. Box 30880 • Santa Barbara, CA 93130
phone: 805-563-2935 • fax: 805-563-2945
e-mail: info4jack@jackcanfield.com
website: www.jackcanfield.com

Who Is Mark Victor Hansen?

In the area of human potential, no one is more respected than Mark Victor Hansen. For more than thirty years, Mark has focused solely on helping people from all walks of life reshape their personal vision of what's possible. His powerful messages of possibility, opportunity, and action have created powerful change in thousands of organizations and millions of individuals worldwide.

He is a sought-after keynote speaker, bestselling author, and marketing maven. Mark's credentials include a lifetime of entrepreneurial success and an extensive academic background. He is a prolific writer with many bestselling books, such as *The One Minute Millionaire, The Power of Focus, The Aladdin Factor,* and *Dare to Win,* in addition to the Chicken Soup for the Soul series. Mark has had a profound influence through his library of audios, videos, and articles in the areas of big thinking, sales achievement, wealth building, publishing success, and personal and professional development.

Mark is the founder of the MEGA Seminar Series. MEGA Book Marketing University and Building Your MEGA Speaking Empire are annual conferences where Mark coaches and teaches new and aspiring authors, speakers, and experts on building lucrative publishing and speaking careers. Other MEGA events include MEGA Marketing Magic and My MEGA Life.

He has appeared on television (*Oprah,* CNN, and *The Today Show*), in print (*Time, U.S. News & World Report, USA Today, New York Times,* and *Entrepreneur*), and on countless radio interviews, assuring our planet's people that "You can easily create the life you deserve." As a philanthropist and humanitarian, Mark works tirelessly for organizations such as Habitat for Humanity, American Red Cross, March of Dimes, Childhelp USA, and many others. He is the recipient of numerous awards that honor his entrepreneurial spirit, philanthropic heart, and business acumen. He is a lifetime member of the Horatio Alger Association of Distinguished Americans, an organization that honored Mark with the prestigious Horatio Alger Award for his extraordinary life achievements.

Mark Victor Hansen is an enthusiastic crusader of what's possible and is driven to make the world a better place.

Mark Victor Hansen & Associates, Inc.
P.O. Box 7665
Newport Beach, CA 92658
phone: 949-764-2640 • fax: 949-722-6912
website: www.markvictorhansen.com

Who Is LeAnn Thieman?

LeAnn Thieman is a nationally acclaimed professional speaker, author, and nurse who was "accidentally" caught up in the Vietnam Orphan Airlift in 1975. Her book, *This Must Be My Brother*, details her daring adventure of helping to rescue 300 babies as Saigon was falling to the Communists. An ordinary person, she struggled through extraordinary circumstances and found the courage to succeed. LeAnn has been featured in *Newsweek Magazine's Voices of the Century* issue, FOX-TV, BBC, NPR, PBS, PAX-TV's *It's a Miracle*, and countless radio and TV programs.

After her story was featured in *Chicken Soup for the Mother's Soul*, LeAnn became one of Chicken Soup's most prolific writers. Her devotion to thirty years of nursing made her the ideal coauthor of *Chicken Soup for the Nurse's Soul*. She went on to coauthor *Chicken Soup for the Christian Woman's Soul, Chicken Soup for the Caregiver's Soul, Chicken Soup for the Father and Daughter Soul, Chicken Soup for the Grandma's Soul, Chicken Soup for the Mother and Son Soul, Chicken Soup for the Christian Soul 2*, and now *Chicken Soup for the Nurse's Soul, Second Dose*.

As a renowned motivational speaker, she shares life-changing lessons learned from her Airlift and nursing experiences. Believing we all have individual "war zones," LeAnn inspires audiences to balance their lives, truly live their priorities, and make a difference in the world. She is an expert in nurse recruitment and retention, and helps to hire and inspire nurses from coast to coast.

LeAnn is one of about 10 percent of speakers worldwide to have earned the Certified Speaking Professional designation.

She and Mark, her husband of thirty-seven years, reside in Colorado where they enjoy their "empty nest." Their two daughters, Angela and Christie, and son, Mitch, have "flown the coop" but are still drawn under their mother's wing when she needs them!

For more information about LeAnn's books, CDs, and DVDs, or to schedule her for a presentation, contact her at:

LeAnn Thieman, C.S.P.
6600 Thompson Drive, Fort Collins, CO 80526
phone: 970-223-1574
e-mail: LeAnn@LeAnnThieman.com
Website: www.NurseRecruitmentandRetention.com

Contributors

Sandra P. Aldrich, president and CEO of Bold Words, Inc., in Colorado Springs, is a popular speaker who wraps humor and encouragement around life's serious issues. She is also the author or coauthor of eighteen books and contributor to two dozen more. She may be reached at BoldWords@aol.com.

Award-winning author **Diana Amadeo** is a busy wife, mother, former registered nurse, volunteer, and freelance writer. Her 400-plus publications include books, anthologies, magazine features, and newspaper articles. She loves the frequent travels and memories with her family.

Annisha Asaph is a graduate of the activation coordinator gerontology program. She has worked in long-term care for three years as a recreation therapist. Her dream is to work for the Alzheimer's Society as a volunteer coordinator. Annisha lives in the small town of Milton, Ontario, Canada, with her husband, Max.

David Avrin is a successful marketing, public relations and branding strategist, professional speaker, and executive coach. Aside from his "real job," he is also the author of the very popular book *The Gift in Every Day—Little Lessons on Living a Big Life* (Sourcebooks, 2006). Reach him at david@visibilitycoach.com.

Aaron Bacall has graduate degrees in organic chemistry as well as in educational administration and supervision from New York University. Three of his cartoons are featured in the permanent collection at the Harvard Business School's Baker Library. He continues to create and sell his cartoons. He can be reached at abacall@msn.com.

Judy Bailey, R.N., graduated from the Hospital for Sick Children, Toronto, Ontario, Canada, in 1967. She has experience in pediatric, surgical, and obstetrical nursing in Barbados, Haliburton, and Lindsay, and is a prenatal educator. As a mother and grandmother she enjoys writing for children and human interest stories.

Nancy Barnes dreamed of being a nurse since she was a child. Most of her nursing career was as an ER nurse. She was adopted at age five and is inspired to write of her experiences as a nurse and mother of adopted twin boys. She resides in Dallas, Texas.

Barbara Bartlein, R.N., C.S.P., is the PeoplePro. She is a professional speaker and offers keynotes, seminars, and consulting to help you build your business and balance your life. She has appeared on *The O'Reilly Factor*, Fox News, and CBS. Her column, "The People Pro," appears in numerous publications. Reach her at barb@thepeoplepro.com or www.ThePeoplePro.com.

L. Sue Booth graduated from St. Vincent's Hospital School of Nursing in Jacksonville, Florida, in 1966, and married Michael, a Nebraska farm boy, a month later. Forty years later, after raising ten children (biological and foster), she is still married, and still an active R.N. serving catastrophically injured individuals.

Ruth Bredbenner graduated form Middlesex County College, New Jersey, in 1978. She is a registered nurse and became certified in oncology nursing. Ruth, now retired, is an active member of Hunterdon County, New Jersey Medical Reserve Core. Ruth enjoys traveling, research, music, and reading and continues to write as inspired. She can be reached at Oliviarn02@patmedia.net.

Kathy Brown, R.N., C.S.P., president of Energetically Speaking, is a motivational humorist, keynote speaker, and author. She has written two books: *Living Happily Ever Laughter* and *I Only Have a Minute . . . So Let's Make It Matter.* Her website is www.kathybrown or e-mail her at kbrown471@aol.com.

Dr. Marlene Caroselli is the author of sixty business books and uncountable articles/curricula. She conducts corporate training and makes keynote presentations. You may reach her at mccpd@frontiernet.net.

Jacqueline Gray Carrico received her associate's degree in nursing, with honors, in 2003. She was an L.P.N. for twenty-six years before she returned to school. Jacqueline is a wife, and mother of a son in college. She was previously published in *Chicken Soup for the Expectant Mother's Soul.*

Tracy Crump graduated from Baptist Memorial Hospital School of Nursing in 1976 and worked five years in the ICU. She has been married to Stan for thirty-one years and has two grown sons, Brian and Jeremy, whom she home-schooled. She now enjoys freelance writing and can be reached at tracygeneral@gmail.com.

Barbara Cueto is worship leader at Coronado Baptist Church in El Paso, Texas. She's authored two books—*From Mafia Princess to God's Princess: A Memoir*, and *Been There, Done That*, meditations for addicts. She lives with her husband, Joe, and their sons, Nicholas and Joey. Contact her at BCuetoMinistries@aol.com.

Ronald P. Culberson, Director of Everything! at FUNsulting, etc., is a speaker, humorist, columnist, author, and former hospice social worker whose mission is to help redefine excellence in health care through humor.

Jeri Darby has been in nursing for twenty-six years. She has been writing for ten years and has over seventy published articles and poems. Jeri enjoys conducting seminars and making inspirational gifts. In the future she plans to write devotionals and Christian romance books. You may contact Jeri at pstopublication@yahoo.com.

Lola Di Giulio De Maci loves writing for children. Her inspiration comes from her now-grown children and the many children she has taught over the years. She enjoys contributing to Chicken Soup for the Soul books and being an inspirational speaker. She writes in a sunny loft overlooking the San Bernardino Mountains. E-mail her at LDeMaci@aol.com.

Kathy B. Dempsey is president of KeepShedding! Inc., a speaking, training, and consulting company that helps individuals and organizations grow and change by "shedding their skin." Kathy is the author of the award-winning book, *Shed or You're Dead: 31 unConventional Strategies for Growth and Change.* E-mail her at Kathy@KeepShedding.com.

Denise A. Dewald writes personal experience articles and poetry for the Christian market. She has been widely published and some of her work has been read on Christian radio stations. She enjoys reading, camping, her family, and her pets. She is currently working on her memoirs. She can be reached at denise_a_dewald@yahoo.com.

Twink DeWitt lives in Hideaway, Texas, with her husband, Denny. Since his retirement, they've served with Mercy Ships and Youth with a Mission for fifteen years. Twink, who helps others improve their writing, especially enjoyed crafting this story about Haiti with her daughter-in-law, Anna. Twink can be reached at tylertex@yahoo.com.

Terry Evans has been a nurse for almost forty years and a writer since she was in high school. She is proud of her profession and for that reason, she writes. Terry wants to share the experiences of her career. She is married and the mother of three grown boys.

Eva Marie Everson is an award-winning author and a national and international speaker. She is the author of the bestselling Potluck Club series *Oasis* and *Sex, Lies & High School.* Her upcoming work includes a book about the Holy Land for Thomas Nelson/Nelson Bibles. Her website is www.EvaMarie Everson.com.

John A. Fagley has been married to his wife, Veronica, for forty years. He is a retired design engineer. He has taught Scripture for twenty-five years at Blessed Sacrament Church in Tonawanda, New York. He has led an in-home Bible study for eight years. He is a cancer survivor, and half the members of the Bible study are survivors also. He can be reached at Johnrayma@aol.com.

Karen Fisher-Alaniz enjoys reading, photography, and vacationing on the Oregon coast. She lives in Walla Walla, Washington, with her husband and three children. She is currently writing a memoir based on her father's wartime secrets and her quest to understand.

Jude L. Fleming holds a master of nursing degree in holistic nursing and a family nurse practitioner degree from Beth-El School of Nursing, University of Colorado, Colorado Springs. She is currently working in the emergency department of a busy city hospital. She spends her winters skiing and her summers hiking, waterskiing, and camping, enjoying the Rocky Mountains of Colorado.

Helen French, R.N., B.S.N., Clinical 111 at the University of Virginia, is a member of STTI International Honor Society, assisted with the H2e Memorandum of Understanding, and in 1989 founded the University of Virginia MERCI Program, which was recognized by State of Virginia Resolution #739.

Patricia J. Gardner received her bachelor of science in nursing from the UT Health Science Center at San Antonio and is certified in hospice and palliative care. Pursuit of a master's degree in English is on hold while she travels for her hospice employer. Pat often finds inspiration for stories in the unsung heroes she encounters while nursing. Besides travel, Pat enjoys reading, movies, genealogy, and hiking. Please e-mail her at pat6@flash.net.

Dr. Val Gokenbach is a vice president and chief nurse executive. She is involved in community initiatives, including the creation of Safety City USA, a nonprofit interactive learning facility for the community. She is widely recognized as an international speaker for her passion for leadership and the promotion of nursing as a profession.

Ivani Greppi returned to college at the age of thirty. In 1992 she received her associate's degree in nursing. Ivani's passions include her family, writing, reading, and traveling. She plans to write the story of her family's conversion to Christianity. Contact her at ivanifh@hotmail.com.

Barbara Haile is a sixty-five-year-old mother of five and grandmother of eight. She has been a professional speaker for the last seventeen years and is a graduate of UpperClass, a Christian leaders and speakers group headed by Florence Littauer. She is acting spokesperson for Happy Hooves, an equestrian therapy organization specializing in disabled children and adults.

Patty Smith Hall received her nursing degree from Kennesaw State University in 1984. Since her recovery, she writes devotionals and Christian fiction with publications in *Guideposts* and *God Allows U-Turns*. Patty lives in Michigan with her husband, Dan, and daughters, Jennifer and Carly. E-mail her at pattynell 2002@yahoo.com.

Gina Hamor received her nursing degree in the Philippines and is on staff at Scottsdale Healthcare Osborn campus. She thanks her late parents, Jose and Delores Hamor, and her dear late foster mother, M. Jesse de Cardy, for their great love and guidance, and for allowing her to see the world. Reach her at ghamor@cox.net.

Jonny Hawkins draws cartoons full-time from his home in Sherwood, Michigan, alongside his lovely wife, Carissa, the CFO of his tiny humor enterprise. They are parents to two young boys, Nate and Zach, and their brand-new baby, Kara, born January 21, 2007. Jonny dedicates the cartoons in this book to Carissa and his little redhead, Kara Elise.

Sue Henley lives in Tennessee. She recently became a widow after twenty-nine years of marriage and has two daughters. She works in a lockdown facility with adolescent boys. She enjoys taking care of others and writing about the lessons she's learned from her patients, family, and friends. E-mail her at doupray2@charter.net.

Cheryl Herndon, C.N.M., ARNP, received her master's degree in nurse-midwifery from the University of Illinois at Chicago in 1991. She has delivered more than 2,000 babies. She has been married thirty-seven years and has five grandchildren. Cheryl is an inspirational speaker and author. E-mail her at Cheryl@womankindservices.com.

A freelance writer, **Margaret Hevel** has had stories published in magazines and books: *Western Horseman, Reminisce, Chicken Soup for the Dog Lover's Soul,* and others. She and her daughter just finished *Parenting with Pets: The Magic of Raising Children with Animals.* Her novel, *The Ivory Elephant,* is on Amazon.com and at Barnes & Noble.

Miriam Hill is the coauthor of *Fabulous Florida* and a frequent contributor to Chicken Soup for the Soul books. Her work has appeared in the *Christian Science Monitor, Grit Magazine, St. Petersburg Times,* and Poynter Online. Miriam's manuscript was awarded Honorable Mention in the Inspirational Writing category of the 75th Annual Writer's Digest Writing Competition.

Sharon T. Hinton is an R.N. and paramedic specializing in parish nursing. Sharon writes fiction and nonfiction and speaks nationally about spiritual journaling and other topics. Sharon lives with her husband and two children on the family farm in rural west Texas. Contact her at sharon@sharonthinton.com.

Beverly Houseman is a retired R.N. and the author of *Rusty and Me: A Mother's Story,* and a contributor to *Chicken Soup for the Caregiver's Soul, Chicken Soup for the Nurse's Soul,* and *Chicken Soup for the Grandma's Soul.* She is a counselor and childbirth educator for a crisis pregnancy center in Kissimmee, Florida. E-mail her at harhouseman@earthlink.net.

Cindy Hval and her husband, Derek, are raising four sons, ages seven to seventeen, in Spokane, Washington. Her work has appeared in *Chicken Soup for the Mother and Son Soul, Chicken Soup for the New Mom's Soul,* and various magazines. She's a correspondent for the *Spokesman Review* newspaper. Contact her at dchval@juno.com.

Thankful for life, **Vanessa Bruce Ingold** gladly shares her near-death experience and all she's learned from it with interested groups. She has many published book articles, including one in *Chicken Soup for the Healthy Soul Living Series: Heart Disease.* She and her husband live in Fullerton, California. Contact her at JCnessa.com.

Daniel James lives with his wife in Colorado. He is an observer of nature and human nature and is cursed or blessed with a dictate to wrestle with the wily word, which one day he hopes to do well.

Ellen Javernick is a second-grade teacher and freelance writer who lives in Loveland, Colorado. She enjoys playing tennis and spending time with her five grandchildren.

Anne Johnson owes all she is to the Lord. Her husband, Matt, is a true blessing as are her two children, Moriah and Christopher. Anne praises God for the ability to be a wife, mother, daughter, registered nurse, freelance writer, and Sunday school teacher.

Kathleen E. Jones is an R.N. and a freelance author. The inspiration for her stories comes from the children she cared for in her twenty years as a pediatric nurse. She facilitates a monthly writing group and is working on a novel about her nursing career. E-mail her at nesjks@juno.com.

Jessica Kennedy received her B.A. from the University of California at Davis in 1995. At 26, she had a brain stem stroke and became a ventilator-dependent quadriplegic. A speaker at classes for respiratory therapists and a writer of inspirational articles, she foresees a bright future. E-mail her at jessica kennedy1971@yahoo.com.

Ruth Kephart works as an R.N. in Pennsylvania and writes poetry and short stories in her spare time. Her poetry has been published in numerous journals and anthologies and she has recently released her first collection of poetry, *For Everything There Is a Season.* Contact her at hoot_owl_rn@yahoo.com.

Jean Kirnak, one of eleven children of homesteader parents in central Montana, attended school in a one-room log schoolhouse. After nursing school graduation, she was an army nurse, then received a bachelor of science degree at the medical school in Portland, Oregon. Since retirement in 1994, she has pursued a writing hobby.

Margaret Lang is an author of twenty-three published stories, a speaker at women's groups, a missionary to Thailand, and a grandmother of two girls. Co-author Nancy Madson is a mother and grandmother and has enjoyed a lifetime of nursing. In her retirement, she rehabilitates wounded dogs at home.

Flo LeClair has practiced oncology and hospice nursing in Worcester, Massachusetts, since 1981. She continues to find it an honor and a privilege to be at the bedside of those passing from this world to the next. Her sense of humor and deep faith are lifesavers against caregiver burnout. Reach her at leclairf@ummhc.org.

Christine Linton celebrated thirty-one years as an R.N. this summer. Her love of writing dates back to high school, when she was editor of her high school newspaper. She is married to Alan, and they have two grown children, Amanda and Michael. She continues to work at Scottsdale Healthcare in the NICU.

Mary Clare Lockman works as an R.N. in a busy oncology/hospice unit. She is the author of a humorous memoir, *Warning! Family Vacations May Be Hazardous to Your Health,* and a children's book, *Barefoot, Shoefoot.* She enjoys family and friends, golf, traveling, reading, and writing. Reach her via e-mail at mclockman @msn.com.

Susan Lugli is a Christian speaker and author. Her stories have been published in *Chicken Soup for the Christian Woman's Soul, Chicken Soup for the Caregiver's Soul,* and *Today's Christian Woman* magazine. She is an advocate for burn survivors and speaks on their behalf. She lives on a ranch in central California. E-mail her at suenrusty@aol.com.

Susan Fae Malkin graduated from nursing school in January 1970, and can't imagine doing anything else! She worked in operating rooms as a staff nurse and an educator. She now works in emergency medicine. Susan has been published in various nursing journals and in *Chicken Soup for the Nurse's Soul.* E-mail her at Harmony51480@aol.com.

Kelly Fordyce Martindale is a full-time publisher, writer, and owner of the Carbon Valley Consumers Report. Many of her published articles and presentations are on women's issues. Kelly coauthored the popular book *Loved by Choice: True Stories That Celebrate Adoption.* She and her family live in Colorado.

Patrick Mendoza has been an internationally acclaimed folk singer and storyteller since 1976. Prior to his career as an entertainer, Pat served in the United States Navy for four years, and worked as a police officer for seven and a half years. Reach him at patmendoza@aol.com.

Maryjo Faith Morgan belongs to the Colorado Authors' League (www. coloradoauthors.org). She hosts a weekly writers' workshop, which furthers members' writing careers. Maryjo produces a wide variety of written work, including business text, magazine features, and creative nonfiction. Her husband, Fred (www.fredsusedwebsites.com), is the webmaster behind www. maryjofaithmorgan.com. They also enjoy tandem biking together.

Emily Morris is a newspaper reporter in Sarasota, Florida. The youngest of Pam and Geoff's four children, she grew up listening to her parents' stories about Vietnam, and is delighted her mom decided to record one of them. Emily, a Penn State graduate, has previously worked as a newspaper reporter in Pennsylvania, Oregon, and Colorado.

Glenna Anderson Muse is a respiratory therapist and writer who lives with her husband, Gene, in Springfield, Missouri. She also has a background in hotel convention planning, and owned her own catering business. She keeps her finger in the cooking pot through a food blog at www.afridgefulloffood.typepad.com.

Tori Nichols is an R.N., writer, business owner, and proud mother. She has worked in pediatrics, orthopedics, surgical, and telemetry, capping it off with a decade in the ICU. Tori lives in southern Illinois with the love of her life. Together they operate Nichols Photography. Contact Tori at www.nicholsphoto.com.

Brian O'Malley is an adventurer, photographer, and professional speaker. His presentations are a masterful blend of adventure and artistry. Brian's presentations have entertained and empowered audiences around the world. From the slopes of Mount Everest to the jungles of Africa, Brian touches the human spirit, illustrating the importance of living life to its fullest. His website is www.BrianOMalley.com.

Kathleen D. Pagana, Ph.D., R.N., inspirational speaker and author, is a professor emeritus and president of Pagana Keynotes and Presentations. Her most requested presentations address Momentum Leadership, the Pursuit of

Happiness, Professional Etiquette, and Time Management. She has written over fifty articles and eighteen books. Please visit her at www.kathleenpagana.com.

Kerry Pardue never intended to become a poet. A medic, police officer, postal worker, and college recruiter, he is a 100 percent disabled veteran who served as a medic in Vietnam. His poems are about recovering from war. They are his road map to a place called *home*. E-mail him at kerrypardue247@yahoo.com.

Mark Parisi's "off the mark" comic, syndicated since 1987, is distributed by United Media. Mark's humor also graces greeting cards, T-shirts, calendars, magazines, newsletters, and books. Check out offthemark.com. Lynn is his wife/business partner. Their daughter, Jen, contributes with inspiration (as do three cats).

Mary Pennington, R.N., CNOR, RNFA, is an OR nurse at Wake Med in Raleigh, North Carolina. She resides in Angier, North Carolina, with her husband and two teenage children. Some of her interests include music and reading. She is actively involved in the nursing organizations, AORN. You may e-mail her at WTPooh9998@aol.com.

Carol McAdoo Rehme never played nurse or bandaged her dolls. Now a grandma, she's relieved to pass the torch of responsibility to the next generation. Carol is a prolific writer, editor, and coauthor of numerous gift books. Her latest project, *Chicken Soup for the Empty Nester's Soul*, will be released in 2008. E-mail her at carol@rehme.com.

James E. Robinson is an award-winning songwriter, successful singer, author, counselor, speaker, and founder of ProdigalSong Ministries (www.Prodigal Song.com). Combining music and educational workshops, he performs in churches throughout the country. In 2003, Jim published his first book, *Prodigal Song: A Memoir*. He lives with his wife and two children in Tennessee.

Karen Rowinsky is a speaker, author, and expert in living life to the fullest. After a twenty-five-year career in women's and community health education, Karen returned to school and earned her master's degree in social work in 2007. Contact her through her website: www.rowinsky.com.

Cyndi S. Schatzman, R.N., M.S., CCRN, a former nursing instructor and critical care nurse, is currently an inspirational speaker and writer. She is married to her college sweetheart, Todd, and has three children that she can wrestle to the ground over candy. Contact Cyndi for your next speaking engagement at mustangok@earthlink.net.

Joyce Seabolt has been an L.P.N. for more than forty years. Her specialties are geriatrics and orthopedics. Among other things, she writes articles for nursing magazines. Joyce lives with her husband, Hal, in charming Red Lion, Pennsylvania. E-mail her at joyceseabolt@hotmail.com.

Frank Serigano received his bachelor's degree in psychology from Binghamton University, his PA Certification from Bayley Seton Hospital PA

Program, and his master's degree from the University of Nebraska Medical Center. He is employed at the Northport VA Medical Center and at the YMCA. E-mail him at fdzi@optonline.net.

Carol Shenold is a freelance writer, teacher, and infection control nurse. She lives and works in Oklahoma City with her daughter and two cats. When she isn't working and writing, she paints portraits and is finishing her mystery novel.

Lillie D. Shockney, R.N., B.S., M.A.S., is director of the Johns Hopkins Breast Center, an oncology nurse, and two-time breast cancer survivor. She has received more than twenty-five national awards related to her work in breast cancer and has written four books and more than seventy articles on the subject.

Susan Stava lives and works as a registered nurse in the Denver, Colorado, area. She celebrates more than twenty years in what she considers to be one of the hardest and best professions in the world.

Delores Treffer received her diploma in nursing in 1969. She practiced as a registered nurse until 1997. After 1997, Delores began a career in medical transcribing. She is married and has two children and one grandchild. She frequently writes short articles for a county newspaper. She enjoys family, friends, and her church.

Judith Weinland Thompson has been publishing how-to articles and short stories since 1988. She has two grown daughters and, having lived as many years in North Carolina as she has in Ohio, fondly refers to herself as a Nutherner.

Kerrie G. Weitzel received her bachelor of arts in English education/psychology with honors in 1971. She is currently working on a novel and a children's book. She has had one book published, *The Innkeeper's Wife*. She lives in Colorado where she enjoys life. E-mail her at twigleaf@frii.com.

Gail Wenos is a humorist, ventriloquist, and president of Gail and Ezra Ministries, Inc. Together, Gail and her dummy, "Ezra," bring touches of love to the elderly. A member of the National Speakers Association, she earned their Certified Speaking Professional designation and received the CPAE Speakers Hall of Fame Award. Her website is www.gailnezra.com.

Judy Whorton received her A.D.N. from Mobile College in 1984. She was employed for fifteen years as an R.N. before retiring. Judy is married to Bob, her husband of thirty-five years. They have two married sons and six grandchildren. E-mail her at whortons@bellsouth.com.

Anne Wilson currently teaches university writing, English, and theater arts courses at several universities in California, but was formerly a nurse among the terminally ill in Albuquerque. Her writings were published extensively in religious/spiritual magazines and journals from 1980–96.

Thomas Winkel and his wife, Nicola, are coauthors of *Transformation from Tragedy: Stories of Hope, Faith & Community After the Tsunami*, an inspiring look attsunami survivors and relief workers. Proceeds support the continuing relief effort in Indonesia. Visit www.WordPointPublishing.com to order.

Wendy Young, M.S.W., C.S.W., B.C.D., is a child and family therapist in private practice in Michigan's Upper Peninsula. She has developed peace and tolerance programming for schools and her local community. She also maintains Kid-lutions: Solutions for Kids, an array of products to assist children with various life problems. Visit her at www.kid-lutions.com.

Permissions

We would like to acknowledge the many publishers and individuals who granted us permission to reprint the cited material.

Hope. Reprinted by permission of Jerline Darby. ©2000 Jerline Darby.

Pilar. Reprinted by permission of Terry Evans. ©2004 Terry Evans.

Memories of Polo. Reprinted by permission of Sharon Tonya Curtis Hinton and the University of Oklahoma, Blood and Thunder Musings on the Art of Medicine ©2004. ©2002 Sharon Tonya Curtis Hinton.

Nurse Nancy. Reprinted by permission of Nancy Jean Barnes. ©2007 Nancy Jean Barnes.

Welcome to War. Reprinted by permission of Emily Morris. ©2006 Emily Morris.

Confessions of a C.N.O. Reprinted by permission of Valentina Gokenbach. ©2007 Valentina Gokenbach.

The Exchange. Reprinted by permission of Cynthia S. Schatzman. ©2006 Cynthia S. Schatzman.

Christmas in July. Reprinted by permission of Kathleen E. Jones. ©2005 Kathleen E. Jones.

Sacred Moments. Reprinted by permission of Judith Lynn Fleming. ©2007 Judith Lynn Fleming.

Nurse, Heal Thyself. Reprinted by permission of Patty Smith Hall. ©2006 Patty Smith Hall.

A Nurse's Touch. Reprinted by permission of Maryjo Faith Morgan. ©2007 Maryjo Faith Morgan.

Finding Christ in a Hospice. Reprinted by permission of John A. Fagley. ©2001 John A. Fagley.

Halloween. Reprinted by permission of Jean Kirnak. ©1997 Jean Kirnak.

Miss Benjamin. Reprinted by permission of Miriam S. Hill. ©2006 Miriam S. Hill.

The Day "Doc" Goss Became a Nurse. Reprinted by permission of Patrick Mendoza. ©2004 Patrick Mendoza.

Goodnight, Harry. Reprinted by permission of Daniel James. ©2000 Daniel James.

Comforter. Reprinted by permission of Cindy Sue Hval. ©2006 Cindy Sue Hval.

Perfect Child. Reprinted by permission of Diana M. Amadeo. ©2006 Diana M. Amadeo.

Child's Therapy. Reprinted by permission of Barbara R. Haile. ©2006 Barbara R. Haile.

Fae Malkin.

The New Grad. Reprinted by permission of Vanessa Bruce Ingold. ©2007 Vanessa Bruce Ingold.

John Doe. Reprinted by permission of Linda Sue Booth. ©2006 Linda Sue Booth.

A Heart for Haiti. Reprinted by permission of Lucie H. DeWitt. ©2007 Lucie H. DeWitt.

MERCI. Reprinted by permission of Helen French. ©2003 Helen French.

A Relay of Control. Reprinted by permission of Florence A. LeClair. ©2004 Florence A. LeClair.

The Tale of the Sale. Reprinted by permission of Kathy Brown. ©2007 Kathy Brown.

The Creepy Visitor. Reprinted by permission of Joyce (Cecilia) Seabolt. ©2006 Joyce (Cecilia) Seabolt.

Janet. Reprinted by permission of David L. Avrin. ©2007 David L. Avrin.

A Lesson in Saying Good-bye. Reprinted with permission of *Nursing2005* journal, Wolters Kluwer Health, Lippincott Williams & Wilkins. ©2005 *Nursing2005* journal.

One Patient. Reprinted by permission of Margaret Krepp. ©1995 Margaret Krepp.

There Is Nun Better. Reprinted by permission of Ron Culberson. ©2007 Ron Culberson.

Fish Therapy. Reprinted by permission of Daniel James. ©2000 Daniel James.

Bridge to a Silent World. Reprinted by permission of Margaret C. Hevel. ©2000 Margaret C. Hevel.

The Survivor. Reprinted by permission of Mary Clare Lockman. ©2001 Mary Clare Lockman.

This Is Bill. Reprinted by permission of Susan Kay Stava. ©2006 Susan Kay Stava.

The Value of Time. Reprinted by permission of Lillian Shockney. ©2006 Lillian Shockney.

Fifty-Fifty. Reprinted by permission of Linda Sue Booth. ©2006 Linda Sue Booth.

A Necessary Change. Reprinted by permission of Anne Christine Johnson. ©2004 Anne Christine Johnson.

Catch of the Day. Reprinted by permission of Carol D. Rehme. ©2000 Carol D. Rehme.

322   PERMISSIONS

The Lifeline. Reprinted by permission of Tracy K. Crump. ©2007 Tracy K. Crump.

My Name Is John. Reprinted by permission of Kelly Martindale. ©2004 Kelly Martindale.

New Life. Reprinted by permission of Thomas Richard Winkel. ©2006 Thomas Richard Winkel.

Sustained Me. Reprinted by permission of Wendy Young. ©2004 Wendy Young.

Optimistic Light. Reprinted by permission of Jessica Kennedy. ©2007 Jessica Kennedy.

God Supplies Angels. Reprinted by permission of Susan Lugli. ©2006 Susan Lugli.

To School Nurses. Reprinted by permission of Ellen Javernick. ©2004 Ellen Javernick.

Angels of Mercy. Reprinted by permission of Lola Jean De Maci. ©2006 Lola Jean De Maci.

To the Nurse Who Served in Vietnam. Reprinted by permission of Kerry Lee Pardue. ©2003 Kerry Lee Pardue.

God's Hand. Reprinted by permission of James E. Robinson. ©2006 James E. Robinson.

Knowing Your Limits. Reprinted by permission of Frank Serigano. ©2002 Frank Serigano.

Thanking Ruby. Reprinted by permission of Jacqueline G. Carrico. ©2002 Jacqueline G. Carrico.

Thank You for Your Care. Reprinted by permission of Denise A. Dewald. ©1993 Denise A. Dewald.